T0356709

Little Vic and the Great Mafia War

Books by
LARRY MCSHANE

Cops Under Fire:
The Reign of Terror Against Hero Cops

Chin:
The Life and Crimes of Mafia Boss Vincent Gigante

Last Don Standing:
The Secret Life of Mob Boss Ralph Natale

Little Vic and the Great Mafia War

Larry McShane

Little Vic and the Great Mafia War

CITADEL PRESS
Kensington Publishing Corp.
kensingtonbooks.com

CITADEL PRESS BOOKS are published by

Kensington Publishing Corp.
900 Third Avenue
New York, NY 10022

All Kensington titles, imprints, and distributed lines are available at special quantity discounts for bulk purchases for sales promotions, premiums, fund-raising, educational, or institutional use. Special book excerpts or customized printings can also be created to fit specific needs. For details, write or phone the office of the Kensington sales manager: Kensington Publishing Corp., 900 Third Avenue, New York, NY 10022, attn Sales Department; phone 1-800-221-2647.

10 9 8 7 6 5 4 3 2 1

First Citadel hardcover printing: March 2025

Printed in the United States of America

ISBN: 978-0-8065-4360-4

ISBN: 978-0-8065-4362-8 (e-book)

Library of Congress Control Number: 2024946553

Whoever brings ruin on their family will inherit only wind, and the fool will be servant to the wise of heart.

—Proverbs 11:29

We're not running away. We're walking.

—John Orena to Colombo family capo
"Wild Bill" Cutolo

Contents

CONTENTS

Little Vic
and Great
the
Mafia War

Darkness on the
Edge of Town

I t was a perfect Long Island evening, with the temperature in the
mid-70s and the promise of another sweet suburban summer in
the months ahead.

Little Vic Orena walked into the warm night air on June 20,
1991, after sharing dinner with a friend inside Stella's Restaurant, a popular spot among the local mafiosi. He climbed inside
his two-door Mercedes convertible and started the engine. A set
of rosary beads hung from his rearview mirror, a gift from his
deeply religious wife's pilgrimage to the tiny village of Medjugorje in Bosnia and Herzegovina—a site where true believers first
reported witnessing visions of the Virgin Mary a decade earlier.

The sky above was clear, but the rising storm inside the
Colombo crime family was once again poised to unleash a tsu-
nami of trouble across its perpetually divided membership.

Orena lit a cigarette with his solid gold lighter and popped
his soundtrack from Broadway's *The Phantom of the Opera* into the
car's tape player before heading out. As the mob veteran stopped
at a red light near his two-story family home in Cedarhurst, Long

Island, he turned his head to the right and noticed an older vehicle with four men inside—each wearing a baseball cap.

The faces beneath the hats belonged to his crime family colleagues. Orena's once loyal associates were now lying in wait for the family's latest acting boss as a growing rift over his ascension to the top sparked a new round of infighting for a mob family already notorious for settling its disputes the old-fashioned way: backstabbing, bullets, and bloodshed.

"They had a hole already dug for his body," recalled his son, Andrew Orena. "And thankfully, my father had a good sixth sense."

Orena, in a lucky and life-saving break, arrived home sooner than the waiting hit squad had expected. Little Vic identified one of the would-be killers as his longtime friend and recently promoted family consigliere Carmine "the Shadow" Sessa.

The would-be assassin had earned his nickname from the Orena sons, who noted Sessa seemed to appear out of nowhere— "Way before his shadow," said Andrew.

The failed scheme was both business and personal. Sessa was once tight with the Orenas—treated like a member of the family, occasionally joining Little Vic for a cup of coffee, freshly brewed for the occasion by the boss's wife inside their home. It was the acting boss who handpicked Sessa to join him atop the family hierarchy.

But Sessa's was not the only betrayal. The Orenas had shared a long and lucrative alliance with the power behind the hit: the legendary and longtime boss Carmine Persico—"Junior" to his allies, "the Snake" to his haters. The two clans were like family outside the crime family, their ties inside and outside the Colombos grown tight across two generations, frequently socializing as sons from both sides followed their fathers into "the Life."

"The Persico and Orena families were as close as you can be in that life," recalled Vic's son Andrew, sitting inside his Long Island home with brother John a full thirty years after the last killing in the war. "My brother John and Michael Persico were business partners and best friends. Michael was godfather to John's son, John Jr."

But stability, never a Colombo family trademark, once more proved elusive for its made members and their leadership in the aftermath of Persico's combined 139-year sentences following a pair of mid-1980s convictions in separate Manhattan trials, with the jailed boss destined to die behind bars yet reluctant to surrender the throne.

And so Carmine Persico, from behind bars, initially appointed an acting replacement before signing off on the recently promoted mobster's murder within two years. Persico then bumped Orena up as the new acting boss, putting the well-regarded and handpicked veteran in charge in a seamless 1988 transfer of power.

It was, for Little Vic, the pinnacle of a career that began decades before as a teen with a zip gun on Patchen Avenue in Brooklyn. And now, three years after rising to the seat of power without twisting a single arm or pulling one trigger, Orena found himself in the crosshairs of the Persico loyalists.

The Snake, indeed. The scenario, if nothing else, offered a perfect illustration of Carmine's hated nickname. Persico was now advocating for his son, Little Allie Boy, to take over as boss upon his upcoming release from prison after an earlier conviction alongside his father.

Sessa, recently flipped to the Persico squad, was particularly motivated by word of a reported plan by Little Vic to assassinate him after a Colombo family induction ceremony to take place the next day. The outnumbered Orena hung a fast U-turn near his two-story suburban home, one hand on the wheel and the other on a handgun, speeding to safety before his hunters could open fire.

There was no doubt where the murder plot originated, an attack marking the end of Orena's decades-long alliance with the Persicos and the kickoff of a devastating internal family bloodletting unseen inside the New York Mafia since ... the last Colombo war, only two decades earlier.

Point Blank

By sunrise the next day, there was word of a second failed plot to execute veteran Orena faction loyalist Joseph Scopo, his life spared only by a last-minute decision to skip a meeting with another gangster inside a mob social club.

One of the hit men drove past Scopo's home in Mill Basin, Brooklyn, and saw the target's car parked safely in the driveway, before all involved in the failed coup gathered inside the Nebraska Diner in Coney Island. Once assembled, the group learned that the Sessa attempt on Little Vic was a failure as well.

The Sessa squad, while awaiting word of the next move, had already fled to a New Jersey safe house, fearful of the mob family's future—and their own.

The Colombo crime family's final round of self-destruction was off and running, a deadly dispute later described in FBI court documents as "a particularly bloody struggle . . . fratricidal bloodletting."

If *The Godfather* offered a romanticized version of mob infighting, with chubby capo Peter Clemenza stirring a pot of sausage and meatballs while the combatants "went to the mattresses," the real thing was considerably more terrifying. The Orena family and their backers abandoned their homes, wives, and kids to find refuge inside safe houses once the shooting started.

The malevolent combatants on either side were soon openly hunting one another on New York streets in a gory conflict defined by betrayal, deceit, and plot twists galore as the faltering Colombos became a house still divided to this day: the Persicos and the Orenas.

Sammy Gravano, the onetime Gambino family underboss turned star government witness, explained the final implosion of the Colombos quite simply in the new millennium: The Commission sent word to Carmine in prison, "You can't go changing guys every 15 fucking minutes. Put the guy in, Vic Orena, he's the (acting) boss."

The approved arrangement imploded on the night of the attempted murder, with Persico's flip-flop igniting a predictable conflict that predictably ended poorly for both sides after another two-plus years of violence.

The lone winners emerged in a torrent of made men on both sides who fled into the arms of law enforcement, their oaths of omertá swapped for plea deals and federal cooperation agreements as they lined up to take the witness stand in multiple prosecutions linked to the war. More than a dozen turncoats flipped before the shooting stopped, with some of the stone killers given a new lease on life after executing their onetime comrades in the street fighting.

Once the shooting finally stopped with a final 1993 slaying, the Orenas (and eventually Brooklyn prosecutors) came to believe the deck was stacked against them by an unprecedented alliance between a veteran FBI agent and two notorious Colombo killers: Lindley DeVecchio, a highly regarded law enforcer, and infamous

Colombo hit man Greg Scarpa, known with good reason among his mob colleagues as "the Grim Reaper."

The story sounded like an implausible pitch for a mob movie, right down to its finale: a shocking finish inside a Brooklyn courtroom long after the shooting stopped. But their too-close ties were real, authorities said, and the shocking relationship would soon become the fodder for a series of books, magazine articles, and—most memorably—the final episode of the HBO mob series *The Sopranos*.

"It was a case of outrageous government misconduct," said Andrew Orena, offering his take on the whole thing. "This thing was way bigger . . . These guys had carte blanche."

Scopo's good fortune expired more than two years later when he became the final victim of a fight with losers on both sides, the literal war to end all New York mob wars, the last of the city's myriad and ultimately pointless internal disputes across the last seven decades of the twentieth century.

"I wound up growing up around a life that was a disease that has destroyed so many families throughout the years, including my own," explained fickle hitman Carmine Sessa after joining the ranks of combatants who found rebirth as government witnesses.

"The movie *Goodfellas* explains it well," said the gangster/informant after admitting to thirteen murders and betraying his ex-friends inside the Orena family. "Meaning, everybody gets killed by a bunch of animals or so-called friends.

"This thing I thought I respected as a young man has no respect. All the families hate each other. And within the families, they hate one another."

Andrew Orena, decades later, still remained outraged by the betrayal of his father by duplicitous gangsters who had once been tight with Little Vic—particularly turncoat Sessa.

"Carmine Sessa used my father's boat more than he did!" he recalled. "He was like my father's son. He had the keys to the city. We were all close with him."

The struggle for supremacy within the Colombo family, like an organized crime version of a *Seinfeld* episode, turned out to be all about nothing.

And Little Vic, a patriarch fighting to preserve the crime family and his own family, wound up losing both after his rise to the top spot. His career highpoint disintegrated into disaster and was followed by a draconian prison term intended to ensure his death inside a federal prison.

Something in the Night

A ndrew Orena recalled lying restlessly in bed on the night of the failed plot targeting his father, afflicted with a vague sense that something inside their world was amiss.

"An eerie feeling," he recalled. "Something was going on. And so I'm in bed, I'm about to fall sleep, I got the lights out. Me and my wife. I had a big night table next to me, with a phone on top. And the phone rings—don't ask me why, I pick it up and I go, 'Is pop alive?'"

The voice at the other end belonged to his older brother, Vic Jr., who assured Andrew their father was indeed alive and summoned him to their parents' house. Andrew, like the others called to the meeting of Orena loyalists, was told to "wear a tie"—shorthand for showing up with a weapon.

Andrew quickly threw on some clothes and grabbed a .9mm Glock handgun, sticking the weapon in his waistband and jumping into his car for a tense ride to his dad's house.

"My wife says, 'Is your father OK?' I said, 'I don't know, I've gotta go to my father's house,'" Andrew recounted, the details still vivid. "We all knew this was part of the life, but we couldn't believe this happened from within, from Carmine—our friend and brother. We were angry, betrayed."

Andrew arrived to find the younger Vic and sibling John already inside their patriarch's Long Island home, where he entered a scene like something out of *The Godfather*, with five Orena faction soldiers standing silent watch outside the residence in the darkness.

"They all say hello to me and gave me a look like it just got real," he recalled. "And one of them says to me, 'Get inside.'"

But his father's front door was locked tight, and he began banging loudly until Colombo underboss Joe Scopo arrived to let him inside after dodging his own bullet.

"He goes, 'Don't worry Andrew, your dad's alright. He's alive.' I go 'Holy shit, what happened?'" he continued. "I go inside and my brothers are sitting at the kitchen table."

The other seats were filled by his father, alongside Orena loyalists Scopo, Pasquale "Patty" and "Wild Bill" Cutolo. It was Little Vic who spoke first: "They tried to kill me tonight." His blue Benz was parked in the garage, the beads still dangling inside, as Little Vic erupted inside the house.

"My father looked at me and said, 'This fucking Carmine! I did nothing but help him and this is our thank you!'" recalled Andrew.

Little Vic quickly asked one of the men to contact the suspected quartet of killers. Anyone who failed to respond was part of the hit squad, he said, before calling for a mandatory meeting of the family leaders one day later to sort things out as the Orena faction headed into deadly territory.

Once the grim sit-down ended, Andrew Orena drove back home for a sleepless night as the Colombo family braced for one final war, a fight for control of a business nearing its expiration date as New York federal prosecutors piled up indictments and convictions against the New York's five crime families.

Vic Orena had instantly become the number one target for his friends turned foes, with the threat of his possible execution hitting his worried sons hard.

"He was the sun that all of us revolved around," recalled Andrew. "I would wait on the stoop of our home every day for him to come home from work as a kid. Like clockwork, he'd come home, and I'd hug him."

But on this night, Andrew's thoughts were darker and more focused on the immediate future than on the past: the attempted coup, the murder plot against his father, and the role of Junior Persico in the failed hit.

"I said to my wife, 'What about the Persicos? Carmine's a snake,'" he continued. "This is on my mind: my brothers are going to get killed. They're gonna lose a decision, and they're gonna get called to go down into a basement—this, that, all these things that we'd see. And listen, it could have went bad. My father and my brothers could have got whacked. And other people did."

Sessa's prominent role was particularly painful, although the Orena son believed his father's life was saved only because the assassin panicked after spotting his dad. "If he just waved and asked, 'How you doing?' it could have been different."

But the discord within the Colombos after Little Vic's rise to the seat of power—with Persico's full support, including a blessing for Orena to both order mob hits and initiate new members into the family—seemed somehow inevitable.

The Snake's extraordinary endorsement for the acting boss saw Orena presiding over a 1988 mob ceremony where associate Alan Quattrache became a made guy—a Goodfella who later flipped and testified against the man who inducted him into the family.

The morning after the failed hit, a still-rattled Andrew awoke and drove to a nearby suburban church, entering the empty house of worship and taking a seat in one of the pews.

"And I'm scared," he said. "I'm scared about the whole thing. And I grab a book of Psalms and say, 'Let me say my prayers.' When I open it up, it's Psalm 56."

Andrew read from its pages, the message inside the holy book eerily apropos for his precarious situation: "Be merciful to me, my God, for my enemies are in hot pursuit, all day long they press their attack . . . They twist my words, all their schemes are for my ruin. They conspire, they lurk, they watch my steps, hoping to take my life."

The younger Orena would emerge over the ensuing decades as his father's biggest postwar advocate, insisting that Little Vic deserved a chance at freedom on two fronts. First, he became convinced the Colombo boss was an unwitting victim in a war fomented by outside forces, including notorious family executioner Scarpa and his longtime FBI handler DeVecchio.

Their alliance would take center stage in the waning days of the war amid allegations the two worked side-by-side on behalf of Team Persico, with DeVecchio eventually facing four murder charges linked to his ties with longtime federal informant Scarpa in a shocking turn of events more than a dozen years after the killing stopped.

And second, in the new millennium, Andrew would wage a fruitless yet ceaseless fight to bring Little Vic home from behind bars, with repeated appeals for his compassionate release from a life sentence imposed after his conviction—with the key witnesses emerging from among his former associates.

Though the Persicos "won" the war, maintaining their tenuous control of the crime family, the flesh-and-blood Orenas emerged as the ultimate victors in the decades after the killing stopped, with Vic's two oldest sons leaving "the Life" for a new life in the legitimate world, the past only a sad and distant memory, and the Persicos barely clinging to their spots atop the foundering Colombos.

The failed murder attempt was followed a day later by a sit-down between the Orenas (Little Vic accompanied by his two eldest sons) and Carmine's brother Teddy Persico, in an effort to restore the status quo and avoid an escalation of the mob family's final and fatal schism.

"My dad told Teddy, 'Listen we have to keep the family together, whatever the beef is,'" recalled Andrew. "You know, like that's that. We've got to stay together here, whatever happens, let's figure it out. But Teddy was adamant, 'Nope, nope, you're down and Allie Boy's the boss.'

"And my father says they're going to have split the family up—'I've got sons, I've got friends in this life. And we know what the outcome is. I'm not having it.' My father said the only one who wins in a war is the government. We'll ruin ourselves. And ultimately, that's what happens."

As the tension mounted, Little Vic stated he would step down as acting boss if directed to do so by Carmine Persico. And Carmine Sessa, representing the Snake's interests, said he was willing to accept Orena's promotion—but only if instructed to do so by the jailed Persico. Instead of détente, the two sides opted for battle.

Blinded by the Light

The latest and last of the Colombo family's incessant internal conflicts kicked into high gear within five months of the failed hit on Orena, after peace talks between the two sides failed miserably.

The lethal 1991–93 Colombo conflict stood apart in the annals of organized crime in the nation's largest city—home to the five mob families forged in 1931 after their first episode of lethal infighting and later host to repeated violent regime changes.

By the end of year one, court papers later recounted, the "Orena loyalists had a standing order to kill anyone who was loyal to Persico."

The approach was par for the course of the New York Mafia. Gambino chief "Big Paul" Castellano was killed in Midtown Manhattan while exiting his car outside Sparks Steak House only nine days before Christmas of 1985, his body left on the street just steps from the entrance and his reserved table empty on the other side of the front door.

Six years earlier, Bonanno head Carmine Galante was executed after finishing lunch on the patio at Joe and Mary's Italian American Restaurant in Brooklyn, one of his trademark cigars still clenched between his teeth. On October 25, 1957, legendary gangster Albert Anastasia was famously gunned down in a barber's chair at the Park Sheridan Hotel after his driver/bodyguard went for a walk.

And, of course, Joe Colombo, boss of the family that bore his name through the ensuing decades, was whacked in 1971 while hosting an Italian American rally in Manhattan's Columbus Circle, yet another example of the family's penchant for self-inflicted wounds.

Carmine Persico would become Joe's replacement two years later, although the Colombos became a family in flux after their new leader's ensuing legal woes. However, their situation was never as bad as that of the foundering Bonannos, who were barred from the Commission and treated as a second-tier operation for a number of reasons, including their infiltration by an FBI undercover known as "Donnie Brasco."

But this conflict was something entirely different inside the crime family notoriously plagued by unrest in its ranks and by regime changes, both violent and frequent.

"EVEN TO THE FIVE FAMILIES, THE FIGHTING COLOMBOS HAVE BEEN BLACK SHEEP," read a *New York Times* headline in year one of the war. The accompanying story by reporter Selwyn Raab offered this take on the murderous mobsters: "Within the violent councils of America's Mafia, authorities say, the Colombo crime family has long been feared as an erratic, troublesome gang."

Combatants were soon lined up behind both Little Vic and his predecessor Persico, who despite his guaranteed death behind bars continued to play a role for his side throughout the latest conflagration. At one point, authorities placed a bug inside the federal prison in Lompoc, California, in an effort to eavesdrop on the imprisoned boss in hopes of gleaning details on possible strategies from his side as the street fight dragged on.

Senior federal court judge Jack Weinstein, in a court document written long after the shooting stopped, offered his take on the violence that took place during the waning days of New York's once mighty mob: "In the closing decades of the last century heavily armed mobs of Mafiosi, protected by bullet proof vests and scanners monitoring police radio channels, roamed the streets of New York in their automobiles (bugged by the Federal Bureau of Investigations) shooting down their rivals in crime.

"One of the more fascinating episodes was the civil war in the Colombo organized crime family."

The battle inside a mob family on the verge of irrelevancy became a tipping point in New York's organized crime history, with the heads of the five local crime families all behind bars within a decade of the battle's final shots.

By then the long arc of the Mafia's dominant role in the life of the city had reached its nadir, its once omnipresent influence disintegrating, now just fodder for federal prosecution and a slew of tell-all mob memoirs penned in the ensuing years.

The combatants on either side laid claim to leadership of the venerable crime family, home through the decades to mob legends such as its eponymous Colombo, the infamous "Crazy Joey" Gallo, the duplicitous "Grim Reaper" Scarpa, and, for a short time, Sammy Gravano, who moved on to bigger and better things alongside Gambino family boss John Gotti, the Dapper Don.

Vic Orena had joined their ranks decades earlier, working his way up to the top spot nearly two decades after his induction as a made man.

"My dad was climbing up the ladder to success and thought he was bringing the family along with him," his son Andrew reflected.

"We thought at the time we were all rising higher, to a better level in this life. But he was just digging us a deeper and deeper hole."

Little Vic, once in the top seat, forged an alliance with John Gotti prior to the war, with the Dapper Don emerging as a backer of the Orena faction in a move to gain control of the open Colombo seat on the ruling mob "Commission" for the heads of the Five Families.

Vic's ascension would guarantee Gotti's plan to control three of the five spots, giving Gotti carte blanch to operate without interference from his haters across New York's mobs.

"John was close with Joey Scopo, the Colombo underboss," explained retired FBI agent Bruce Mouw, onetime head of the Gambino Squad. "He used to come to John's club. And Scopo's best friend was Gene Gotti—they even had a loan-sharking business together. And Gotti had no love for Persico."

But Gotti, he recalled, had little affection for anyone unless it served his purpose: "He hated everybody. He would go down to the Ravenite (social club) and call the Colombos 'the Cambodians'—always fighting."

The move by Gotti, already a mob star in the media and head of a powerful family, was typical of the blustering boss. The Gambino head was enjoying a winning streak in his ongoing battle with prosecutors, earning his nickname "the Teflon Don" by beating three consecutive prosecutions as headlines detailed the boss's swaggering rise in the wake of his hit on Castellano.

"I FORGOTTI!" read one headline after Gotti walked on a 1984 charge of beating a mechanic in Hells Kitchen, with the victim insisting from a witness stand two years later that he did not recognize the man who assaulted him.

A 1986 racketeering prosecution fell apart after Gotti paid $60,000 to one of the jurors. And he was acquitted four years later in the shooting of a Carpenters Union leader. The brash Gotti had predicted as much: "3-to-1 odds I beat this case."

He did, too.

The Colombo war eventually stretched across parts of three years, with the high-profile Gotti eventually behind bars for a 1992 federal court conviction as the carnage raged into the next year: eleven bodies scattered in and around Brooklyn, with another twenty-eight combatants wounded before the shooting came to a finish.

Authorities arrested 123 fighters from both sides before the peace was restored, with 61 from the Orena faction and 60 from their opponents; 75 of the combatants were prosecuted for their crimes.

"The Persicos technically won," said Mouw. "But the winners and the losing side, they still got killed. The federal government wins."

Andrew Orena offered his own take on the war, citing the rise of Carmine Persico as evidence of the overall decline of the leadership across the Five Families.

"Persico wasn't an old-world Sicilian but a feared street thug," he explained. "Very smart, but treacherous and a feared boss. No loyalty and lacking the fatherly love that a boss should have for the family. Persico was not a fatherly figure like a Carlo Gambino, Joe Bonanno, or 'Tony Ducks' Corallo. Cosa Nostra means '*our* thing,' not '*my* thing.'"

Hit squads from the Persico side, the most notorious and successful of which were led by Scarpa, were soon cruising the streets inside a station wagon turned lethal arsenal, filled with an assortment of shotguns, rifles, and pistols tucked inside hidden compartments, as they hunted anyone associated with the Orena faction.

The Orena side responded in turn once the war began, with their friends turned foes scoring a pyrrhic victory once the handcuffs went on the warring mobsters and the shooting finally stopped in 1993. The last murder came months after the war had apparently ended, the final volley inside the imploding Colombos.

The most prominent figure emerged as Scarpa, a terrifying and legendary mobster with a history as a stone-cold killer dating back to the 1960s and reportedly responsible for double-digit homicides across a Mafia career that included two secret stints working for the FBI.

He was brought back into the fold for a second time in 1980 by the highly regarded DeVecchio and worked as a mob mole for the next dozen years and throughout the war. He was linked to four killings—more than any combatant.

DeVecchio worked as the lone handler for Scarpa after the two teamed up in an unusual arrangement between agent and informant. Scarpa hid in plain sight as the war raged on, inexplicably and brazenly flying beneath the government's radar—or so it seemed.

"His charmed life vis-à-vis law enforcement," declared court papers filed after the war, "may be attributed to the fact that he was a longtime informer for the FBI."

Ex-Colombo family capo Michael Franzese, long after leaving the world of organized crime, once observed that Scarpa took pleasure in his lethal role: "He enjoyed doing the work." His zeal extended beyond the ranks of organized crime. Scarpa once allegedly arranged the murder of a Manhattan doctor as a favor for a girlfriend.

Though court papers noted that the Persico faction was just one-third the size of the Orenas, the outnumbered crew managed to fight above their weight as the conflict raged. And acting boss Little Vic, his family, and mob loyalists became convinced, quite presciently, that the odds were stacked against them.

Not until the shooting ceased would the Orenas learn about the hard-to-imagine alliance between DeVecchio and Scarpa. The mobster and his FBI handler were in frequent contact throughout the Colombo conflict, with DeVecchio later described by a fellow federal agent as behaving like "a cheerleader" for the Persico faction.

The once revered DeVecchio would become the target of investigators inside the FBI and the Brooklyn prosecutor's office, his reputation tarnished by the allegations despite his unshakable insistence to this day that his relationship with Scarpa was strictly business.

Prosecutors would eventually allege that the Grim Reaper's wartime free rein on the street, with his front-and-center role in the bloodshed on the streets of Brooklyn, was aided by his unlikely FBI partner.

"We're going to win this thing!" said an animated DeVecchio at one key point during the conflict, stunning his FBI colleagues—including younger agent Chris Favo—with a declaration they interpreted as rooting for the Persico side's victory.

His memorable one-liner was eventually immortalized in court testimony and later resurrected in an episode of *The Sopranos*, the TV series about a fictional mob family operating across the Hudson River in New Jersey.

"Lin got too close to Greg," said former federal prosecutor John Gleeson. "And when guys pointed it out, really good agents, to me that was a very good lesson in you've got to be very careful about handling key informants. And Lin got too close."

The long-retired DeVecchio, speaking seventeen years after his Brooklyn prosecution for assisting in a quartet of mob-linked murders collapsed like a house of cards, reasserted his innocence and blasted his critics in a recent interview from his Florida home.

"I meant we, meaning the FBI, were going to take down a family," said DeVecchio. "To this day, I'll never understand the conclusion in Favo's twisted mind, a way to stick it to me. My beef was with the Brooklyn DA. I remember thinking, 'You assholes, there's plenty of exculpatory information about me.'

"And yet they went ahead with the trial. The whole thing was ludicrous on its face. I had to laugh. [District Attorney] Joe Hynes—self-serving horseshit."

But Andrew Orena remains convinced to this day, after taking his own deep dive into what happened once the shooting stopped, that the mob bloodbath was absolutely fomented by the FBI agent and his prized, if unlikely, mob mole.

"The FBI knocks on everybody's doors and says, 'There's a hit on you' or 'there's a war going on' or 'you're a target' or this and that, what do guys do?" asked Andrew. "They either do one of two things: they go, 'Yeah, I need your help' or they say, 'Let me get a gun.' They create fear. And that's how the Colombo war started."

Gravano, the former Colombo soldier who became a Gambino underboss and then a devastating federal informant, recalled the insanity of the whole conflict, that lethal exercise inside a Mafia already well past its prime.

"The Colombos couldn't get away from the act of shooting each other, lying and bullshitting, getting into a war again," said Gravano. "I knew Vic well, and he seemed like a very good guy, a fair guy. I didn't think he was trying to take over the family. It sounded like made-up bullshit. He had two sons in the life who stuck with him.

"In the end, they had enough of this fucking Persico and all this other bullshit and they went to war."

Gravano dismissed the rumors that Orena was intent on moving from interim boss to family boss as initially overstated. The decision for his promotion was, in fact, intended to restore some stability to the family in the absence of Persico.

But stability was always elusive inside the Colombos, once parodied as "the gang that couldn't shoot straight" in a book by that title by late and legendary New York columnist Jimmy Breslin.

Let's start at the top: Notorious boss Persico, who put the war in motion with the failed Orena hit as Colombos sorted out their deadly differences one last time. A 1976 FBI document described Persico as more than suited for his long-distance role in the conflict, with a turncoat mobster citing the gangster as "well-deserving of the nickname 'Snake.'"

And his son, "Little Allie Boy," who was locked up when the war began and would remain in prison for more than thirty years after briefly taking the helm from his father after the war ended.

The mob scion's pending freedom from an earlier conviction alongside his dad had already complicated things between the two sides by the early 1990s, with Persico intent on bumping his jailed son up to replace Orena once back on the streets.

Family bosses Gotti, Anthony "Gaspipe" Casso, and Vincent "the Chin" Gigante were ultimately dragged into the mob's last open shooting war.

The Orena faction similarly featured Little Vic and his two eldest sons, along with the aptly named "Wild Bill" Cutolo and veteran loyalists like "Nicky Black" Grancio—two Orena backers who would eventually pay for their allegiance with their lives in a pair of gruesome killings.

Federal prosecutor Ed McDonald, at the time of the war, explained the self-destructive fighting simply: "It was very important to Carmine Persico to have his son or (future boss) Andrew Russo in charge."

While Persico-backer Scarpa emerged as the deadliest force in the fighting, the details of his life inside "the Life" and in the embrace of the feds were only fully exposed after his 1994 AIDS death from a tainted blood transfusion.

His decades of work for the FBI were ultimately detailed in an avalanche of unsealed documents dating to the Kennedy administration.

Scarpa was paid a total of $158,000 across the years for his work as a mob mole and operated under a previously unseen arrangement with federal investigators. First, he would never be called to testify at trial, an almost standard part of any cooperation agreement. And second, his identity would remain a secret to all, including to federal prosecutors making cases off his information, an arrangement previously granted only to the most crucial of informers.

The mobster identified as "34," the number on his FBI file, was also collecting $253 in monthly Social Security benefits from the federal government. He in turn began referring to DeVecchio as "the girlfriend" or "Mr. Dello" during their phone conversations, and the agent was repeatedly welcomed into Scarpa's home for chats around his kitchen table.

The Grim Reaper's actual girlfriend, Linda Schiro, was frequently privy to the conversations between the pair.

Little Vic, swept away by the waves of organized crime turncoats, was convicted and sentenced to die behind bars, sold out by his former colleagues to become the biggest pelt of the war. Once Orena landed in prison, a steady stream of combatants shared their tales of the war when they appeared on the witness stand, in a plethora of podcasts, or via book deals, their vows of mob secrecy a thing of the past.

DeVecchio wrote one, too, a 513-page tale subtitled *The Shocking Frame-Up of a Mafia Crimebuster*. It opened with his account of sitting in disbelief, handcuffed inside the Brooklyn district attorney's office, having gone from being a crime-buster to just a perp.

The Orenas, across the next three decades, struggled both for their father's freedom and for their own survival as memories of the war receded in the new millennium. His two oldest sons, after following their dad into the Colombos, faced their own criminal charges, including a stunning prosecution where allegations of the collaboration between DeVecchio and Scarpa led to the Orena sons' acquittals.

The siblings still wound up behind bars on other charges before eventually returning home and turning their backs on the mob.

Andrew Orena, in the aftermath of his family's life in organized crime, delved into the details of exactly what had happened during the conflict and remains convinced DeVecchio and Scarpa collaborated in turning the heat up.

"I saw what they did," he said. "Every time there was peace or peace talks, somebody would get shot. It was, and I'm telling you, there were days out there where it was like a ghost town. And then you would see a Persico car. You would spot a group of guys.

"And then somebody would get shot at or killed. It was like they parted the waters and paved the way on certain days for these guys."

The hard feelings lingered long after the shooting stopped. A decade after the war began, the wife and son of vanished Colombo family captain Cutolo flipped to become government witnesses against the missing man's alleged killer. Persico's son, Allie Boy, was eventually convicted of the murder.

Andrew Orena, in reassessing the self-destructive battle between the Goodfellas, remains convinced the real tale of the Colombo's demise was dramatically different from the one presented to jurors.

"There's this very generic story out there that's been presented by the government," he said. "That my father tried to take over the Colombo family from Carmine Persico. It was all nonsense, all bullshit. Everybody has their own truth, and that was not our truth. I decided to hold on to our truth."

My Hometown

Victor Orena Sr. was the grandson of Sicilian immigrants, old-world furniture makers who found a new home in Canarsie, Brooklyn. The family name was actually Arena, but it was mistakenly altered by a sloppy transcription at Ellis Island in 1898. And their new home, unlike the Canarsie of the twentieth century, was a largely rural area, flanked by Jamaica Bay.

The recently arrived family opened a successful furniture store and settled into their new surroundings in their new city. The change of their surname was etched in stone with the death of patriarch Salvatore, whose grave marker was simply inscribed ORENA.

Vic was the older of two sons born to John Orena, who was nineteen when he married fifteen-year-old Ruth. Much as his own sons would worship him, young Vic—born August 4, 1934—adored his father while growing up. Tragedy struck in the form of the tuberculosis epidemic, with the immigrant Orena family devastated by the then fatal disease.

Among those stricken was Vic's dad.

The father and his older son became inseparable in John's final days, with Vic grimly standing vigil as his dad's condition worsened.

As the family story goes, John called out in Italian for his son to bring him a glass of water. By the time Vic returned, the father had changed his mind. John explained that he was just visited by a woman, dressed all in white, who materialized in his bedroom window and spoke to him directly.

It was the Virgin Mary, the dying father declared, pointing with a trembling finger at the spot where she had appeared.

"Where you are going, you will never be thirsty again," declared the ephemeral vision. John related the story with his last words, closed his eyes, and died. The wake was held in the house, and Vic slept in the bed with the corpse until his dad was taken for burial.

The four-year-old boy blamed the woman in the window for taking his father away.

The young widow was left with Vic and his kid brother, Mickey. Her in-laws turned on the suddenly single mom, who was no longer welcome in Canarsie. And so the trio moved to Bedford-Stuyvesant, a far more crowded urban neighborhood, where the Orena spread gave way to an apartment at 66 Patchen Avenue. The lonely mom, now on her own, soon took up with a local hoodlum—a married guy and a made member of the Profaci family, and their romance soon led to complications.

Death followed young Vic once the new kid on the block became fast friends with twelve-year-old Paul McLaughlin, a classmate at Our Lady of Good Counsel parochial school, who had also lost his father to an early demise. The pair jumped a free ride on a passing trolley car. As the two seventh graders hung from the back of the trolley, McLaughlin leaned to the side on a street lined with parked cars. His head slammed directly into one of the vehicles with a loud thump.

The young Orena "jumped off the car, assisted him to his feet and the two walked away," reported the *Brooklyn Daily Eagle* in a story headlined "BOY, 12, HITCHING ON TROLLEY, DIES IN FREAK ACCIDENT."

Vic was even more stand-up than the ancient newspaper story indicates. The boys were riding with some other friends when the fatal accident occurred. The only one to stay and help the mortally injured Irish kid was young Vic Orena. But McLaughlin collapsed a short distance away, with a passing driver loading the injured youth into his car and speeding to Brunswick Hospital.

The boy, his skull fractured, died a few hours later.

Vic's efforts failed to pacify the school principal, who called out her student at a school assembly: "This tragedy would never have happened if Paul avoided hanging out with hoodlums like Victor Orena."

The investigation into the death led to a sit-down between authorities and Vic's Italian-speaking grandmother Rose LaBella, who decided the truth was the best way to go. Vic's mom skipped out on the session, and the outraged Rose laid the whole mess at the feet of her absentee daughter.

"It's not his fault," she declared in accented English. "He gets it from her! I don't know what to do with the both of them!"

Vic, already branded a chronic truant, knew instantly that his chance of emerging unscathed was gone. Two things happened: First, he was dispatched to the Lincoln Hall reform school before his fourteenth birthday. Second, a lifelong animosity toward his mom began festering inside the teen.

"A classic case of Sicilian Alzheimer's: you forget everything but the grudges," noted Andrew. Vic was off to the reformatory in suburban Westchester County. The sentence likely saved his life, even as it put him on a course that provided both his deliverance and ultimate demise.

"If he didn't spend the time he did there, he most certainly would have died before getting out of his teens," said Andrew. The wayward young man received the sacraments of communion and confirmation, tentative steps toward the Catholic faith that he blamed for his father's death.

And then his kid brother, Mickey, came to visit with a story about their mom and her gangster boyfriend. By now, she and the handsome mobster were parents to a baby girl—a complication that led to more complications. After one particularly explosive argument, Vic's mom called her lover's wife.

The next time the now-enraged mobster visited the Orena home, he was armed with a knife and sliced up her abdomen and face in a violent rage. The jailed Vic felt helpless at hearing the story but plotted his revenge.

On the day he exited Lincoln Hall, at age sixteen, Orena arranged to pick up a zip gun from a local pal. Armed with the single-shot homemade weapon, he stalked the streets of Bed-Stuy hunting the boyfriend.

He found the man sitting behind the wheel of his car, stopped on the street. Young Orena bolted for the vehicle, gun in hand, heading directly for the driver's side window and firing the single bullet at the stunned target's head—only to watch as the projectile grazed the man's skull and slammed into his shoulder.

Orena started swinging, landing punch after punch to the man's face as he tried to drive off. Each blow came with the same shouted warning: "You ever touch my mother again, I will fucking kill you!"

The kid scored a one-sided victory. "My father beat the shit out of him," said Andrew Orena. But the triumph appeared to come with a cost.

The mobster went immediately to his capo with his tale of the attack on a made guy—a made guy!—by a local street punk. The capo reached out to Vic's uncle, and the teen was brought before Profaci skipper Sebastian "Buster" Aloi inside his social club headquarters.

Aloi first delivered a harsh tongue-lashing to the young man, loudly explaining the laws of the street and the need to respect his elders—especially those inside "the Life." Orena understood but refused to give an inch.

"If he ever lays a hand on my mother again, I will fucking kill him and bring his head back here," said Orena in the old family story shared by his son Andrew. "And I don't give a fuck about the consequences."

Aloi couldn't help but admire the balls of the teen, and there was soon consideration of bringing him into the family as a made guy despite his tender age.

"They wanted to straighten out my father when he was sixteen years old," said son Andrew, "but the books were closed. Anyway, Buster loved my father from that day on. And when my dad walked out of the club, all the guys with the fedoras tipped their hats as a show of respect. My father loved that."

The fatherless young man found his mentors inside the Brooklyn social club, a group of older men who offered instructions on life in general and life within the Mafia in particular. He proved a respectful student, keeping his ear opens and his mouth shut while ascending through the ranks.

His connections to the Aloi crew were strengthened when his aunt Gina married bookmaker Nicky Melia, a first cousin to Buster. He also forged a bond with the capo's son, Vinnie, who followed his father into the Colombo family.

There was also, as the decades passed, his flesh and blood family: devoted wife, Joan, and their five sons, born in the same Brooklyn neighborhood where Vic came of age decades earlier. Little Vic would loom large in the lives of his boys, in ways both positive and problematic, as he climbed up the mob ladder in the coming years.

Future Colombo boss Carmine Persico and fellow Brooklynite Vic became friendly as Orena was eventually inducted during a 1973 ceremony, after the family "opened the books" to accept new members.

The revered and respected Carmine stood for the new initiate. At one point, Orena appeared poised to become a capo himself but was passed over for the elevation of Persico's son, "Little Allie Boy," and instead Vic was assigned to the young gangster's crew. The mob veteran shrugged off the slight, his commitment to the Colombo family still rock solid.

"Allie was making like my father was going to be captain," said Andrew. "But it would make sense that the father would make his son the guy. You know, (they) were in the drug business. My father was adamant, that's where he drew the line. He was like a money lender who wouldn't lend money to bad gamblers. He figured it would only make it worse on them."

That same year, Orena was identified as the chauffeur for one-time Colombo acting boss Joe Yacovelli, with a mob turn-coat reporting that Little Vic had attended a Nyack, New York, meeting where the murder of Joey Gallo was discussed. Rumors surfaced years later when the last Colombo war began that he was possibly involved in the hit.

"My father wasn't a part of that, but I'll tell you what: my father knew of the planning of that," said Andrew.

Despite the initial resentment over Allie Boy's promotion, Vic became a mentor to the younger mafioso, much as Carmine had been to him. Orena shared his low-key and level-headed approach to mob business with Allie Boy.

It was a style that served him well: Orena's rap sheet included only a pair of arrests for perjury and gambling, and his lone stint behind bars was for four months in a Long Island lockup for loan-sharking.

"My father spent time with Little Allie and had some influence in raising him in the Life," explained Andrew. "Carmine Persico saw my father as a loyal, intelligent, trustworthy, and capable ally. And Little Allie had both the traits of his father and the style of my father."

When Carmine Persico was first imprisoned in the early 1970s, for hijacking and loan-sharking, Orena landed with the crew of underboss Vincent Aloi, Buster's son. Reports indicated that the pair's illicit earnings came from, among other things, loan-sharking, union labor, and the Garment District in Manhattan, as Orena became Aloi's right-hand man on the streets.

"They sat down together all the time," said one official about their close ties. "Aloi and Orena were big earners and very popular with Persico."

By July 1983, Little Vic's promotion had come through: he was identified as a Colombo family capo underboss Persico. An FBI document one year later confirmed that Junior remained as the boss, with his son Little Allie Boy as the consigliere, even as the elder Persico's legal woes continued to mount.

"My father knew these guys, my father did whatever he did," said Andrew. "But he was more of a businessman. I shouldn't say that, but he got into trucking, the air freight business. He used to go to work every day to an office."

The ties between the two clans were further tightened when John Orena went into a lucrative trucking business with Carmine's son Michael. The two were making millions of dollars with their Kennedy Airport–based operation, and the pair grew closer than brothers as their business flourished.

"The best of friends," recalled John. "And we built that business up. And I had other friends who went into the business and became very successful. We used to profit about $1 million a year. We did a lot of airport business. I got up every morning and went to work."

When John's namesake son was born, Michael Persico stood as the baby's godfather.

"The two families were close, no doubt," recalled onetime Colombo capo Franzese. "No doubt. Allie Boy's and Vic's sons were close. But Vic wasn't family."

Vic Sr. eventually opened the door wide enough for his oldest sons to walk through and join the Colombo family. "He groomed each son according to our different personalities," recalled Andrew decades later.

When Johnny and Vic Jr. followed their revered father into the world of organized crime, it was the younger of the two, the father's namesake, who entered first.

Vic Jr. "was always on the path," said his sibling John. "He really didn't have any direction but that life. Vic was always fighting, and my father let him be that. He was a partner with my father in the shylocking business.

"Vic was hotheaded. If you said the wrong thing to Vic— maybe because he was short—Vic was an animal. Vic was ferocious. I'd equate him to [boxing legend] Roberto Durán."

Even kid brother Andrew recalled there was something different about Vic Jr.

"Vic is super intelligent, very smart, well spoken," said Andrew. "But he had that edge. Everybody would say, 'I get along with your brother John, but I'm a little afraid of Vic.' Those eyes!"

John Orena soon followed into the ranks of the Colombos, with Vic slotting him in the crew run by capo Teddy Persico, who was known to the five Orena kids as Uncle Teddy.

"Teddy was a sweetheart of a guy," recalled Andrew. "Teddy made John an acting capo in his crew, and the two were always together."

The roaring '80s were initially the best of times for the Orena family, now living their version of the American dream in an exclusive section of suburban Long Island, as the good times rolled inside and outside Little Vic's world.

Ronald Reagan was in the White House, New York Mets stars Doc Gooden and Darryl Strawberry were on the field in Shea Stadium, future New York Giants Hall of Famer Lawrence Taylor was in the Meadowlands. Cocaine was everywhere, and televisions were tuned to the newly launched music channel, MTV.

The Berlin Wall came down and director Martin Scorsese joined Robert DeNiro in reintroducing America to boxer Jake LaMotta in *Raging Bull*. It felt like the future was bright and the skies all blue for the Orenas, who were blissfully unaware of the dark future looming in the decade ahead.

Vic Jr. was already running a multimillion-dollar loan-sharking operation with his dad, along with a lucrative gasoline bootlegging operation. John's trucking business with Michael Persico was going full tilt at Kennedy Airport. The future was bright. Andrew was engaged to future wife Denise, and his parents were already doting on six grandkids.

But the middle Orena son never joined his siblings inside the Colombo family as a made guy, his ascension nixed by his mom.

"Benny Aloi said to my father, 'We should bring Andrew in,'" recalled the unmade man. "I was part of everything for sure. But my mother made my father promise her no more of her sons will get brought into that life. He promised her that he wouldn't."

The friendship between the Orenas and the Persicos would shatter once Little Vic was targeted for death, with Sammy Gravano charging that the fickle Carmine Persico turned to violence after his attempts to remove Little Vic by other means failed following Orena's 1988 promotion.

"When Persico couldn't do it through the Commission, he wanted to kill Vic," recalled Gravano, noting that Gotti had enough votes to veto any attempt to oust Orena. "That's the norm for him. And they went on a hit, and they pulled up by his house. And they blow the hit."

The failed murder attempt targeting Little Vic was standard procedure inside the treacherous Colombos, as John Orena noted decades later.

"What other families had wars?" he asked. "It's basically the Colombos, three times. And the last one was the worst. There were a lot of casualties. You know who was a component of that? Greg Scarpa. And he was a major asset. They paid this guy for years.

"So the war in my eyes was twofold. It was one of the most violent and notorious wars. And it was the last one."

It was only Vic's prescient wife, Joan, the yin to Vic's yang, who felt the dangerous undertow that threatened to sweep the family away after her husband's ascension inside the Colombos. The deeply religious Irish Catholic, with four of her sons named for Christ's apostles, made her peace with the trade-off.

The loyal wife began attending daily Mass and joined a prayer group to pray the rosary daily, then made a trip with one of her daughters-in-law to visit a holy site in Bosnia and Herzegovina.

"My mom had mixed emotions about Pop's promotion," said Andrew. "She was always conflicted about that life to begin with. My father lived by the rule of an old-world Sicilian lifestyle and its code like a true zealot. And my mother's life was dedicated to prayer and the practices of the Roman Catholic Church. But her husband took that path, and she was dedicated to him and her sons."

His rise to the top was reason for excitement among his boys, offering their dad his shot at the brass ring and a spot on the Mafia's ruling Commission alongside the heads of the other four families.

"We were proud of our father and knew he would do a great job," recalled Andrew. "New doors would be opened in business. Power and respect were all part of it. We believed his new position would take us to a place of generational wealth."

The future seemed wide open as Vic assumed his position atop the Colombos, with his third son recalling that the bump was initially a cause for celebration—with one caveat.

"Jail was always an issue, something that was a possibility," Andrew said of those first heady days. "But generally speaking, my father wasn't a loud, boisterous guy. He wasn't getting into fistfights. He was low-key, and we really had a lot of confidence in him, that he could manage the family. And when they brought him in to be acting boss, it was just what he wanted. We were happy."

6

Growing Up

Though the Orenas never discussed the topic of the Mafia around the dinner table, the brothers found it impossible to ignore some of their father's closest friends. Among the most memorable were Tommy DeSimone and Jimmy "the Gent" Burke—a pair of Lucchese family associates who became pivotal figures in the infamous $6 million Lufthansa heist, prominently featured in Martin Scorsese's classic mob movie *Goodfellas*.

A long-ago photo captured Vic stuffing envelopes with cash as DeSimone and Burke look on approvingly, long before the two were played by Oscar winners Joe Pesci and Robert De Niro.

"With the Lufthansa heist, I was actually working in the airport at that time," recalled Johnny. "I'll never forget, they had a drawing of the guy they said was in on it. And my father, he goes, 'Who does that guy look like?' And it was Tommy. They were following Jimmy everywhere. He used to say, 'Let me buy these guys a drink with some of my money from Lufthansa!' He was a crazy guy."

The Orena sons, from a young age, became friendly with the mob visitors to the family home. Andrew recalls one afternoon when he sat on the stoop waiting for his dad and DeSimone popped by to visit.

Things went sideways from there, and the ensuing and surreal scene morphed into something both unlikely and unforgettable.

"I told him my dad was still at work," recalls Andrew, a sense of wonderment still in his voice. "Tommy says, 'What's the matter? You look a little down.' Well, the pretzel guy—like an ice cream truck, but with pretzels—came by, and he went down the block, and he wouldn't stop for me. Tommy goes, 'C'mon, get in the car.'

"He throws the car in reverse, and he backs up and cuts the pretzel guy off. I'm sitting in the front seat, and I see Tommy jump out of the car and he slaps the guy. And he's choking him, and he comes back with an armful of pretzels.

"He tells me, 'Don't worry. Every day, when you're out there, he's gonna stop for you. And don't give him no money! He's not going to take your money.' I think the guy never came back! But that's Tommy DeSimone."

There were other hints of their father's secret life: DeSimone, after a heist of some sort, showed up with alligator shoes for John and Vic Jr. On another night, DeSimone took the two oldest Orena boys on a field trip.

"He walked us into a place called the Action House—[Lucchese capo] Paul Vario had something to do with it," remembered John. "They had half-naked go-go dancers in cages, wearing boots! I couldn't have been more than eight, nine years old."

On another memorable evening, Burke came by the house to meet with Vic Sr. and they headed off together for the Feast of San Gennaro, an annual Little Italy celebration controlled by the Genovese family. When the boys awoke the next morning, their room was filled with toys won from every game of "chance" at the feast.

"My brother Vic thought Jimmy was just pretty good at the games," recalled a smiling John.

The benevolent side of Burke was tempered mightily by the mobster within. Mom Joan Orena once mentioned a problem with a neighbor across the street, and Jimmy the Gent sprang into action.

"He broke all the Christmas lights at the house and started throwing them at the front door," said Andrew. "After that, my mother wouldn't even tell him if she had an argument with anybody on the block."

And there was a later trip to Little Italy by Andrew and John, accompanied by their pal Michael Persico, for a meal and a few laughs. One of the group took notice of an attractive dancer performing inside the club.

"We're hanging out and drinking, and the girl pulls [one guy] up and we're dancing on the stage and everything," said Johnny. "And the lights go on, and a guy says to Mike Persico, 'Somebody wants to see you guys over at the bar.'"

When they arrived, they were greeted by a Queens gangster named John Gotti.

"I didn't even know who he was, and this was way before the limelight: John Gotti!" says John, chuckling at the recollection. "He goes, 'I saw all of you dancing, I'm gonna tell your fathers.' Then he bought us a drink and everything."

They later discovered that their father helped the Dapper Don develop his fashion sense.

"You remember the ties he used to wear, with the matching pocket squares?" asks John. "You know who bought those all for him? My father. He had them custom made. All those ties that John Gotti wore later on, when you saw him really sharp? My father bought him those ties. He used to get them every Christmas."

When the heat inevitably amped up over the Lufthansa heist, Little Vic was called in to discuss a mob hit on Burke. His son

Andrew recalled how his dad and two older siblings were initially considered to handle the killing before the plans eventually changed.

"They wanted my father to kill Jimmy in his house, in Cedarhurst, because Jimmy trusted my father," said Andrew. "And they were going to use Johnny and my brother Vic to be there, just to make Jimmy feel safe. And Jimmy would have got killed in the basement. My father was distraught over it.

"But it turned out Tommy took the brunt of it, because he was supposed to get made and that was never going to happen. When Tommy disappeared, I'll never forget that, you know?"

DeSimone's murder was reportedly handled by the Gambino family, with Henry Hill of *Goodfellas* fame insisting in 2007 that the execution was personally seen to by a young Gotti. In Hill's account, DeSimone was shot three times in the head, and his corpse was never recovered.

A second account later emerged, laying the blame on Burke for the hit, alleging he took care of DeSimone after a Lufthansa worker identified his partner in crime from an old mug shot. That version had the same ending: Tommy's final resting place remained an eternal mystery.

The Irish American gangster died of cancer while behind bars in April 1996, following his conviction for the murder of a drug dealer.

As Vic Sr. moved up the Colombo ranks, he did what any successful businessman would do: He found his family a nice home in the suburbs. The Orenas relocated to Long Island, swapping Bed-Stuy for upscale Cedarhurst—a square-mile slice of Nassau County settled before the Revolutionary War. It was a nice change of pace for Little Vic's sons; brothers Johnny, Vic. Jr., and Andrew shared a single room, while a fourth son slept in a room with their parents.

The tony enclave, one of the area's wealthy "Five Towns," was named for the grove of trees near the old village post office. The family, instead of living in two cramped bedrooms, now resided in a beautiful two-story house.

"Cedarhurst was a very beautiful town with wealthy people," recalled John with a chuckle. "We always found the worst kids."

Vic Sr. made a smooth transition into his new world, although his sons began hearing whispers about dad's real business. By the time the oldest boys were in high school, their father was both driver and trusted confidant for underboss Vincent Aloi.

"It wasn't like today, when guys walk around a certain way and you could say, 'That guy's a gangster,'" said Andrew. "People just knew he was something different. Growing up, kids would say to us, 'Is your father in the Mafia?' To be quite frank, I didn't know there was a Mafia. I thought these guys, Tommy or Jimmy, they were our uncles.

"And my father would always say, 'If anybody asks you that question, just say it's baloney. It's not true. There's no such thing.' So I was a zealot! I'd say, 'No such thing!' I didn't really know as a kid that there was a Mafia."

John, as the oldest, started to figure things out—and his father, as the boys grew older, acknowledged what John had long suspected about his dad's secret life outside the law.

"When we were kinda young, we knew," said John. "I think he finally needed something to talk to us about. So if he said he didn't like somebody, of course we didn't like them. And if he liked somebody or he looked up to somebody, or he used to tell stories about that person, we looked up to them like they were God. That's just the way it was.

"My father didn't want us to behave like idiots; he wanted us to act like men. And he did that until we were grown men. So if you talked too much, you got a look. If you drank or started getting a little tipsy or mouthy, he'd say, 'Enough. No more.'

"You couldn't even pick one grape from a bunch if you were sitting at a table with other men—you had to take a whole twig, or that was a dishonor. I didn't even know! Maybe one day a guy pulled one grape and they figured out a reason to kill him—he's no good!"

New York City Serenade

From the launch of New York's Five Families, the Colombos were perpetually quickest on the draw when it came to internal conflict, and home to three familial bloodlettings between 1960 and 1992 alone. The Brooklyn-based crime family's lineage dates to the Castellammarese War of 1930–31, with Joseph Profaci emerging as the first boss of the Colombo family.

Profaci arrived in New York as one of 2,240 passengers aboard a ship dubbed the *Providence* that departed Palermo, Italy, on August 1, 1921, and arrived at Ellis Island three days later. His ferocity was belied by his less-than-imposing stature: the Sicilian immigrant stood just five foot six and weighed 178 pounds. The new arrival declared his intentions to become an American citizen and permanent resident of New York City, leaving behind his old-world legal problems (including a forgery charge).

Yes, Profaci said, this was his first time in the Big Apple. And no, he declared, he was not an anarchist nor a polygamist. He planned to move in with a cousin on Elizabeth Street in Manhattan. He became an American citizen on September 27, 1927, and, after settling in Brooklyn, soon assumed his slot as one of the five original Mafia family leaders.

According to reports, the Colombo boss operated what was known as the "Italian lottery" and was arrested on a charge of "being a suspicious person" alongside gangster Joseph Magliocco during a mob sit-down at a Cleveland hotel in December 1928. The two were dressed for success and taken into custody while wearing suits and ties.

Like the fictional Don Corleone, head of the mob family in *The Godfather*, Profaci ran his faction and a legitimate importing business that led to him being known with some renown as the "Olive Oil King." Over the next three decades, he became a major mob player and lived in a Bensonhurst mansion. And he was among those in attendance at the infamous 1957 Apalachin Meeting, an upstate New York gathering of the mob's top figures that was famously busted by state troopers.

Profaci, along with three fellow mafiosi, was taken into custody after authorities stopped his 1957 Oldsmobile. He was later called in by state investigators and invoked his Fifth Amendment rights to all questions about the infamous gathering.

His domain included the Brooklyn waterfront and the drug trade over which he remained unchallenged until the Gallo brothers targeted him in 1960, led by the colorful "Crazy Joey"—known for keeping a mountain lion inside the basement of his Red Hook residence.

In a dispute over a bookmaking operation, the Gallo crew kidnapped Profaci's underboss—his brother-in-law Magliocco—and future family boss Joseph Colombo.

The nickname despised by Carmine Persico—"the Snake"— was perfectly illustrated when he switched sides in the Gallo-Profaci war of the early 1960s, turning on Joey and his brothers, Albert and Larry. The future boss, reputedly working as a mole inside the Gallo crew, was privy to the other side's war plans before one of the most infamous botched hits in the history of organized crime.

The young Persico, in a murder attempt later resurrected for the Francis Ford Coppola mob movie classic *The Godfather*, was among the Profaci boosters in attendance when a garrote was wrapped around the neck of Larry Gallo inside the Sahara Lounge in August 1961.

The victim survived when a beat cop, wondering why the bar was open on a Sunday, walked into the would-be execution as his partner waited outside in their car. The fleeing suspects shot the second officer in the face as they bolted from the bar, and the unconscious Larry Gallo, once awake, predictably refused to identify his attackers to police.

The original plan, according to decades-old FBI documents, was to kill Larry Gallo and two other loyalists and for all three bodies to disappear. Step two would be a phone call luring sibling Joey to a sit-down under the pretense that his brother was there—and then whack him as well.

The hit team had decided the garrote was a better idea than a plot to "gun them down and leave bodies all over the streets. . . . The plan was just to have them disappear and never been seen again." With the targets "all free on bail at the time, it would be felt by the authorities that they were jumping bail."

The same paperwork showed Persico had also reached out to recruit Scarpa for the Gallo cause, with the Grim Reaper declaring that "he knew the Gallos were crazy and that nothing but trouble could come from joining with them; therefore, he would not consider leaving the organization to associate with the Gallos."

The Gallos were reportedly responsible for blowing up Persico's Cadillac in 1963. Seven years later, Persico declined to respond when asked by a state committee on organized crime if he was behind the attempted bar murder. It was one of seventy-one times that Persico invoked his Fifth Amendment rights before leaving.

The internal strife ended with Joey Gallo's conviction and lengthy imprisonment for extortion and Profaci's death from natural causes in 1962, but the family rift continued, as they became known as the Colombos following the installation of a new boss.

Joseph Colombo, the head of the family that came to bear his name, learned the seat of power came with a price after his 1964 ascent to the position quickly made him a target of federal investigators. Within three years, Colombo was featured in a *Life Magazine* mob story on the Mafia. The heads of the Five Families became convinced the piece was planted by the FBI, but there was no doubt that Colombo had landed on the law enforcement radar.

In July 1968, Colombo was arrested with fellow bosses Carlo Gambino and Angelo Bruno of Philadelphia inside the House of Chan restaurant on loitering charges that were quickly dropped. Colombo's response to the increasing law enforcement attention was unprecedented and more than a little odd: two years later he founded the Italian-American Civil Rights League, headquartered inside the Park Sheridan Hotel in Manhattan.

On June 29, 1970, tens of thousands of supporters turned out in Columbus Circle for the nascent organization's first rally, where singer Jimmy Roselli performed for the crowd. Some two thousand of the assembled then marched in anger to the FBI office, scuffling with cops in an attempt to storm the building before the situation was defused.

Among those in the crowd that day were Little Vic Orena and his sons.

The new group raised a reported $600,000 from a Madison Square Garden fundraiser five months later, with Frank Sinatra and his pal Sammy Davis Jr. as the headliners. All seemed right for Colombo—at least until Joey Gallo walked out of prison on March 19, 1971, intent on undercutting the boss's reign.

There were, by then, a number of Colombo critics voicing their displeasure with the boss, including Frank Majuri, underboss of New Jersey's DeCavalcante family.

"How can they make a guy like Colombo sit at the Commission?" he asked boss Simone DeCavalcante in a wiretapped conversation.

Colombo was mortally wounded in a wild public hit before ten thousand eyewitnesses during a Columbus Circle rally sponsored by his organization in June 1971. The killer was a Black man posing as a press photographer. The shooter in turn was gunned down immediately after blasting Colombo, never getting a chance to explain his "motive."

Decades later, in a long story in *The New Yorker* magazine, Colombo's son Chris declared that the rumors that Crazy Joey was behind the hit were totally off base, insisting his dad was a victim of the FBI's COINTELPRO, a program launched in 1956 to disrupt the Communist Party's activities and later expanded to target other groups.

"Trust me, Joe Gallo did not kill my father," said Chris Colombo, alleging that the FBI offered his dad a deal before the hit. "They told him, 'Step down. You won. We'll never pinch you again.'"

Colombo turned down the offer and was soon gunned down, and his son was convinced the feds were behind his murder.

"It was a conspiracy," said Chris. "I have researched it quite good."

His take on things rang true with Andrew Orena, a fellow son of a Colombo family boss. As Orena investigated after his dad's conviction, he discovered disturbing parallels between the handling of his father's case and the FBI's much-maligned and ultimately disbanded program used to infiltrate the Communist Party, the Ku Klux Klan, and the Black Panthers between 1956 and 1971. The operation folded amid charges of widespread abuse, particularly for trampling on civil rights, and for the use of paid informants to infiltrate and disrupt the targeted groups.

Greg Scarpa, for instance.

Andrew's digging after the 1990s war convinced him there was more to the infighting that landed his dad behind bars, insisting that DeVecchio worked behind the scenes with Persico loyalist Scarpa to ensure Persico's victory and the inevitable demise of the Orena faction.

Gallo would eat his last meal while celebrating his forty-third birthday late on April 7, 1972, at Umberto's Clam House in Little Italy. The flamboyant mobster was shot three times before he staggered outside and collapsed on Mulberry Street. In a strange twist of fate, he was outlived by Colombo. Joey, paralyzed and unable to speak, lingered for seven years and passed away in May 1978. The Gallo hit became part of mob lore. The hit team's identities were never confirmed, and the execution was later re-created for film in Martin Scorsese's mob epic *The Irishman*—with actor/comedian Sebastian Manascalco playing the part of "Crazy Joey."

Little Vic was by then ascending the Colombo ladder—he had been induced into the family shortly after the Gallo murder.

In an odd twist of fate, Vic Orena owed his late 1980s ascension as Colombo head to mob-busting US attorney Rudolph Giuliani, a fellow Brooklynite from a family of Italian heritage. The high-profile prosecutor made front-page news after declaring war on the Five Families, while he pondered a future in politics.

The ambitious young federal prosecutor and future mayor, a son of both Brooklyn and a dad with a criminal rap sheet, was appointed in June 1983 as chief prosecutor for the Southern District Federal Court in Manhattan—one of the most prestigious jobs in law enforcement.

The young Giuliani quickly focused his attention on the Mafia, on New York's mob fiefdoms reaping millions of dollars in crooked cash, their reach extending from the concrete in the skyscrapers to the clothing in the Garment District and from sports gambling to corrupt city officials.

The mob-buster's father had once done jail time for an armed robbery, a detail uncovered by the late journalist Wayne Barrett. Barret alleged that several of the mayor's cousins were involved in organized crime in the borough, and the mayor acknowledged that his parents moved to Long Island to keep their son away from the local gangsters.

So there was a personal note to Giuliani's decision to take on the city's deeply entrenched Five Families in an unprecedented targeting of the Mafia. And he went after the mob bosses and their top colleagues with a new tool: the federal RICO act, which opened the door for prosecutors to tie together unrelated crimes to show patterns of racketeering, convictions for which came with stiff penalties.

Giuliani's targets included Carmine Persico and the heads of the Genovese and Lucchese families, all of whom were tried in what became known as the "Commission trial." In a shocking decision destined for defeat, Persico took a star turn as his own lawyer during the trial at the Manhattan federal courthouse.

A family boss leading his own defense against the feds was unprecedented, and many of Persico's mob colleagues were stunned by his decision. John Orena once posed the question to the brother of powerful Genovese boss Vincent "the Chin" Gigante.

"I was in jail with the Chin's brother Mario," recalled John. "And I asked Mario one day, we were talking, and me and Mario were very close. And he wasn't too friendly with too many guys. So I said, 'Let me ask you, Mario, how did Junior become able to be his own lawyer? I mean, you guys are right there, with your brother and everybody else on the Commission—they're going to let this guy be his own lawyer?'

"And he said, 'That's a long story.'"

Brilliant Disguise

At first glance, Carmine Persico did not cut an imposing figure: standing five foot six and weighing about 150 pounds, he was slight man. But he became a familiar and ominous presence in his native Brooklyn, typically dressed in a coat and tie on the streets of Red Hook, Carroll Gardens, and Bensonhurst.

By the time of his death in 2019, Persico's rap sheet included an eye-popping twenty-five indictments—some of which disappeared, along with potential witnesses.

The precocious future mob boss and high school dropout, eventually known to Colombo loyalists as Junior, emerged as a violent force at an early age. He was first arrested in 1949 after a fight on the boardwalk in Coney Island and was scooped up by police a year later after a battle between two local gangs in Prospect Park left a teen combatant dead from a gunshot wound.

Though initially busted as a material witness, Persico was eventually charged for lesser crimes tied to the brawl. The young gangster, inducted into the Colombos at the exceptionally tender age of twenty-one, quickly became notorious in Brooklyn and beyond. Two infamous tales illustrate Persico's cold-blooded policy of death sentences for those who ran afoul of the mafioso.

The first came after a car ride with renowned horse racing jockey Albert Grillo, known as "the Blue Beetle," on February 23, 1951.

Grillo was driving a car carrying seventeen-year-old Carmine and older brother, Alphonse Persico, along with an enemy of the siblings from an earlier dispute, in which Junior was shot in the leg. As they drove through the Brooklyn night near the Gowanus Canal, passenger Steve Bove was shot and killed and his body dumped in the gutter, where a passerby found the corpse hours later.

"As we were riding along, I heard a shot," the jockey testified. "I saw Allie [Alphonse] putting a gun at Steve's head. Steve was slumped down. He kept shooting, three or four more times. He told me, 'Drive where I tell you, or I'll kill you too.'"

Though Carmine was initially charged in the murder, Allie Boy wound up taking the weight for the gruesome execution. To dodge a death sentence, he pled guilty and was slapped with a twenty-year prison stretch. Star prosecution witness Grillo wisely relocated to California.

Fast-forward seventeen years: Grillo returned to Brooklyn in December 1968 and never made it back west. The old jockey was shot four times inside a Long Island social club only three days before the New Year.

And there was the tale of Tony "the Gawk" Augello, a thirty-year Colombo veteran who ran afoul of Junior after taking Junior's son, Little Allie Boy, to a drug deal in the 1980s. The hulking mobster, six foot three and 250 pounds of intimidation, had gone into hiding after skipping out on a parole violation hearing. Augello's decision was apparently motivated by the mere thought of Junior's wrath for his role in the case.

Augello resurfaced on May 9, 1983, and convinced his son-in-law to meet him in Long Island. The two drove through the suburbs, and the fifty-nine-year-old gangster asked the younger man to drop him off at a Burger King, where Augello could use a pay phone to make some calls.

Augello told his son-in-law to return in thirty minutes. As the young man headed off, Augello dialed home to say goodbye to his wife and daughter. He did the same in a second call to his attorney. Then he hung up the phone, put a .357 Magnum revolver in his mouth, and pulled the trigger rather than face Persico's payback for dragging his son into the drug business.

Three years later, a federal sentencing memorandum alleged that Persico played a role in two of the most spectacular Mafia hits in history. Persico was on the hit squad dispatched to gun down boss Albert Anastasia in a notorious October 25, 1957, execution inside the Park Sheraton Hotel in Manhattan. Anastasia was famously whacked while waiting for a shave inside its barber shop, and the four-man assassination team was later dubbed the "Barbershop Quartet." The paperwork alleged that Persico shared the information with a relative.

The killers were never arrested, and underboss Carlo Gambino became boss of the crime family that still bears his name.

The same document implicated Persico in the 1972 execution of Joey Gallo, his reputed partner in the murder of Anastasia. The paperwork alleged that the Snake orchestrated the slaying of his former associate after becoming convinced Gallo was responsible for the shooting of Joe Colombo. It was a strange bit of payback, as Gallo had refused to testify when called by authorities investigating the infamous Anastasia whacking.

Persico had dodged a literal bullet of his own during the family's 1961 bloodletting, when he was shot and wounded in the left hand. The gangster never regained full use of the hand. But he was already on the radar of law enforcement, his criminal profile rising as his ascension inside the Colombos continued across the ensuing decades.

Persico would land in the boss's seat following the Colombo hit on June 28, 1971, taking over while the shooting victim lingered for another seven years. An October 1975 FBI report advised that "Persico, for all practical purposes, is the boss of the Colombo family.... Reliable informants have described Carmine Persico as a vicious killer who has personally participated in many murders over the years."

By then, Persico was facing a plethora of legal woes—starting with a long-running prosecution dating to 1959 for allegedly orchestrating the hijacking of $50,000 worth of linen from a truck.

He was eventually tried four times. Two prosecutions ended in mistrials, and two more resolved when convictions were overturned on appeal. A fifth prosecution finally led to a 1969 conviction that left Persico free on bail pending yet another appeal, when he was arrested on state charges of operating a multimillion-dollar loan-sharking operation.

He was cleared on that charge after a bizarre trial in which the presiding judge closed the courtroom to the media and the public over concerns that coverage of the case and his mob ties could influence the jury against the defendant.

A brief respite from prison ended after his 1981 bust for a parole violation and conspiracy to bribe an agent from the Internal Revenue Service for information about probes into the Mafia.

He spent three years behind bars and walked free in March 1984. But he was soon on the FBI's Most Wanted List and on the lam after a law enforcement source tipped Persico about an upcoming federal indictment, causing the boss to bolt.

Persico was arrested eleven months later, after a family relative collected a $50,000 reward for revealing Junior's hideaway inside his Long Island home.

A key witness in his prosecution, in an early sign of the mob's changing world, emerged as Jimmy "the Weasel" Fratiano, a seventy-two-year-old turncoat gangster who admitted to five murders and sparred with defense attorneys.

"Aren't you really lying about being a tough guy and a murderer?" came one pointed query from defense lawyer David Breitbart. "Isn't all that testimony you've given about yourself just a joke?"

Fratiano's response was quick: "You want the names? All gangsters, not innocent people."

In June 1986, Persico was convicted as boss of the Colombos for extorting millions of dollars from city construction businesses and unions and received a sentence of thirty-nine years imposed by Manhattan federal court judge John Keenan. Little Allie Boy was convicted alongside his dad and sentenced to twelve years.

"Mr. Persico, you are a tragedy," Keenan told Persico at sentencing. "You are one of the most intelligent people I have ever seen in my life."

The next indictment came just three months later, an unprecedented federal racketeering case targeting the highest levels of New York's crime families. Persico made the equally unprecedented move to work as his own defense attorney, a ploy that allowed him to challenge the government's racketeering and murder conspiracy case without actually testifying under oath.

In his emotional closing argument inside the Manhattan federal courtroom, Persico called on the jurors to return an acquittal after a ten-week trial. His wife and four of their children sat listening as Junior fought for a long-shot victory in a trial where jurors heard from 85 witnesses, listened to 150 wiretap recordings, and viewed more than 500 surveillance photos.

"Put aside any preconceptions or prejudices you might have about the Mafia," said the fearsome boss, his Brooklyn accent echoing in the courtroom throughout the ninety-minute summation. "Membership alone is not enough to be a crime . . . Mafia, Mafia, Mafia! Take Mafia out of this trial and there's no case here."

The polite mob chief paused briefly when a female juror sneezed during his closing and offered her a smile and a "God bless you." He argued that the massive case compiled by prosecutors lacked any "direct evidence" against him and bemoaned the government's "despicable" turncoat witnesses, including the relative who ratted him out.

"When does it end, when does it stop?" he asked the jury in his summation. "When do they leave you alone?"

Codefendant Anthony "Tony Ducks" Corallo, reputed boss of the Lucchese crime family, offered a glowing one-word description of his colleague's performance before the bench: "Wonderful."

But on November 19, the jurors repudiated Corallo's review, returning a guilty verdict. A one-hundred-year sentence imposed two months later ensured the defendants would die behind bars. Yet the venerable Mafia don was not ready to surrender the Colombo family reins and remained atop the family to promote Orena two years later, before changing his mind and announcing his preference for the imprisoned Allie Boy.

The latter trial served as a wake-up for New York's Five Families that the times were changing, and the mob took steps to protect themselves in the new era of turncoats and the devastating new federal Racketeer Influenced and Corrupt Organizations Act, with its draconian jail terms.

Andrew Orena recalled members of the New York crime families attending a Brooklyn sit-down with their attorneys after the sentence was imposed on Persico to discuss the new statute.

"A lot of guys were there," he said. "Associates and whatever. It was businesspeople. It was a nice event, because that's when the whole idea of the RICO enterprise law was going to be an issue in the future. That's basically how we took it, but business as usual.

"And our opinion was maybe the next tier was a little more careful, cautious, a little more underground. And it was . . . But it definitely changed the mind's eye to the dangers of being the boss."

9

Jungleland

Vic Orena's ascension to the seat atop the Colombos, in addition to eventually putting him in the crosshairs of federal authorities, came with a land mine even closer to home. Carmine "the Snake" Persico continued to hold on to his position as leader, and his presence, even from prison, loomed large inside the family.

And the Orenas, better than most, were aware of their old friend's reputation for conniving and backstabbing. Little Vic's own rise to the top, approved by Persico, was preceded by the execution of his predecessor.

"Carmine and (son) Allie Boy were one hundred percent gangsters, and diabolically brilliant," said Andrew. "But you know, unfortunately, that life breeds contempt and treachery."

Destined to die far from the Brooklyn streets, Persico initially installed Colombo veteran Jimmy Angelina as acting boss in his absence. The mob veteran, a friend of Michael Franzese and reputed mob executioner, took over in the summer of 1986, receiving instructions funneled to him by the jailed boss's sibling, Teddy.

Little Vic, promoted to captain three years before, wound up as Angelina's successor shortly after his predecessor was demoted and then executed in a typically treacherous bit of Colombo business.

Benny Aloi was named the new underboss in a changing of the Colombo guard in which Angelina was initially knocked down to consigliere. Angellina didn't last long in his new role once Orena took over: DeVecchio reported in late November 1988 that Angelina was "recently hit," on orders from Persico.

The same paperwork said Orena and Aloi "were fully aware" of the killing, and an FBI document confirmed that Little Vic backed the whacking of a colleague who spent just fourteen months atop the Colombos.

On November 28, 1988, Angelina was lured to his death by a mob colleague who picked the victim up outside his Garment District office for a final ride to Kenilworth, New Jersey, and the suburban home of a fellow made man.

The driver pulled into the garage, and the target exited the car and walked up the stairs inside—only to find Billy Cutolo and Carmine Sessa waiting for him. The garage lights went dark and the killers blasted their old colleague.

Angelina's body was buried after the killers cleaned up the crime scene. The details of the murder were eventually shared when one of the participants turned into a cooperating witness.

Different explanations for the hit emerged: Angelina was making a power move on his successor Orena to regain his position atop the Colombos. Or, as Sessa testified after flipping to the feds, the victim was whacked for skimming money from the family.

Either way, Vic Orena was now in charge of the family.

"Persico ruffled a lot of feathers doing that," DeVecchio said of the Orena promotion. "And Orena had worked for years for him. It's good to be the king, a good deal. And Persico gave him a lot of authority, with the Commission and the OK to kill. But a lot of the guys who'd been there a long time were not happy about taking orders."

The same FBI document, later released as part of Scarpa's federal file, offered this take on the transition of power: "Source advised that it was Gambino boss John Gotti who forced the Colombo family to appoint a permanent hierarchy so they could sit down with the other families. The source said that the 'acting' designations are a formality in view of the incarceration of Junior Persico."

It was a shrewd move by the Dapper Don, assuring him of a key ally aboard the ruling five-man Commission.

Orena was indeed well respected and trustworthy, a mob veteran who managed to avoid prosecution almost entirely during his time on the street. He was a good earner, a loyal capo, and a Persico ally, who made sure the jailed gangster's family kept collecting its percentage of the Colombos' income, said the Orena sons.

There were some grumblings that the acting boss was only inducting loyalists from his native Queens, spurning the Brooklyn membership once in power. But with the new order in place and the Colombos moving forward under their new leader, the future appeared bright and wide open.

"When they brought my father in to be the acting boss, it was just what he wanted," recalled Andrew Orena of his dad's new position. "And we were happy for him reaching the level he wanted to attain. He built the family back up to something significant again, and he didn't do it with a hail of bullets."

Little Vic was barely a year into the job when things changed on November 13, 1989, with the brutal execution of a made Long Island mobster and Colombo veteran named Tommy Ocera.

The Rising

O cera was a well-known entity inside the crime family and the co-owner of the mob-friendly suburban restaurant the Manor. Regular customers included Little Vic and his two eldest sons. Fellow Colombo associate Michael Sessa was inducted during a ceremony at the catering hall and restaurant in Merrick, Long Island.

Ocera, in the years before joining the Colombos and rising to captain, was a former prize fighter. In addition to welcoming an assortment of Goodfellas at his eatery, he ran a loan-sharking operation and owned a piece of two illegal gambling clubs.

Things went sideways for Ocera on October 5, 1989, when Suffolk County police raided his restaurant and departed with the owner's damning record books, including one with names, numbers, and debts owed by some of his customers.

The rattled mafioso, accompanied by his girlfriend, Diane Montesano, paid a visit to the local cops four days later in hopes of recovering the books only to find the police were holding on to one filled with his handwritten notes on assorted illicit loans. The paperwork could also implicate Little Vic and Patty Amato in the loan-sharking.

On his way home, the unnerved Ocera stopped at a local bar to knock back a startling five martinis while pondering the prospects of his future after the potentially fatal faux pas. Orena's sons stopped by Ocera's restaurant a day later, asking to see Ocera. Montesano checked with her boyfriend before driving them to a meeting at his home.

Ocera later received a pair of contradictory anonymous phone calls, court papers showed: one urged him to flee and the other warned he was a dead man.

Little more than two weeks after the raid, the couple left the Manor around 1:30 a.m., after closing up. Montesano carried the night's proceeds and each climbed inside their own cars. Ocera typically followed Montesano home to ensure her safety. On this night, she noticed two cars parked across the street near a Long Island railroad station, long after the trains had stopped running.

Neither vehicle, she noted, had a license plate.

As Montesano drove into the night, she later testified, one of the cars appeared and veered head on at her vehicle. As the car passed under a streetlight, she recalled getting a good look at the driver's face.

She would later pick the man out of an array of Colombo family mug shots and testify that the driver resembled Greg Scarpa Sr.

A bizarre chase ensued. Montesano drove onto the sidewalk to make her escape. When she finally caught up with Ocera, he climbed into her car, and they drove to an all-night diner.

Vic Orena popped into the Manor the next night and talked to the couple about the bizarre incident. Little Vic joked with Montesano about her driving skills, and she recalled that he appeared cordial and nonthreatening during their conversation. Montesano last saw Ocera on the night of November 12, when the couple visited a small club to watch a pianist from the Manor perform a solo gig, after which Ocera drove her home.

And no one, other than his killers, ever saw him alive again.

A confidential FBI document based on information from a redacted source one month after the killing confirmed the execution of the missing Ocera, who was taken for a final ride that ended with his murder, a metal wire wrapped tight around his throat.

The details behind the killing emerged over time, including the role of Gambino head John Gotti in allegedly recruiting his new fellow boss, Orena, into the plot.

The hit plan, as later alleged, was hatched inside Gotti's headquarters in Manhattan's Ravenite Social Club, with the Dapper Don asking Little Vic for vengeance against Ocera in the killing of mob associate Greg Reiter, whose father was a close friend of Gotti's.

It was an agitated Gotti who welcomed Orena to his lair for a private sit-down. The Gambino boss appeared far more serene after their deadly discussion. According to Sammy Gravano, Gotti was "ripping mad about this Ocera" before his meeting with Orena about handling the situation.

The session both improved Gotti's demeanor and sealed Ocera's fate as the Colombo boss allegedly signed off on his first hit as acting head of the family.

"John came back calm," recalled Gravano, and he later told Sammy that "they whacked that Tommy Ocera."

Authorities alleged Orena, in addition to appeasing Gotti, had his own reasons for the killing: a confidential witness told investigators that Ocera was skimming cash collected from a private sanitation company, cutting the boss out of his share.

The Colombo head ordered associate Jack Leale to handle the hit during a clandestine meeting. Co-conspirator Michael Maffatore later testified how he overheard Little Vic's direct order for the murder: "I want this thing taken care of."

Leale emerged from the sit-down and boasted to his brother-in-law, Harry Bonfiglio, that he "just got the contract to whack Tommy Ocera."

Maffatore then drove Leale to one of Ocera's gambling operations for a meeting with future Colombo underboss Pasquale Amato. The driver later recounted the family leader's instruction that "they didn't want (Ocera's) body to be found."

On November 13, 1989, Leale summoned the doomed gangster to a meeting with Amato inside the latter's Long Island home. The mobster jumped Ocera and held him down as Leale wrapped the garrote around his throat and pulled the wire tight.

The killers tossed the corpse into the trunk of a car driven by Bonfiglio for a last ride to Queens and buried the body two feet below ground in the borough's Forest Park. The driver was later caught on a wiretap griping that he was never paid for his work, including digging the grave.

"All the way from Long Island to here with a stiff in the back, a murder victim," whined Bonfiglio. "Hundred fucking years I woulda got for that. They would have melted the fucking key."

Amato, a regular visitor to Ocera's restaurant, failed to appear there the next day—or ever again. Leale assumed ownership of the victim's two gambling clubs as payment for his work. Years later, court documents revealed that Ocera had made a final appeal to Leale: the victim wanted his corpse left in a location where the body would be found, allowing his widow to collect the insurance money—a dying request that was ignored.

Lucchese family veteran Little Al D'Arco, after later flipping to testify for the feds, revealed that Little Vic informed him at a December 1989 holiday dinner for the Colombo and Lucchese family leadership that he had ordered the murder as a favor to Gotti, waving his hand toward to ground to illustrate that the body had been buried.

The Colombo boss added, "We gave him a *luparo bianco*," ensuring the corpse would never be found, he said.

The vow provided untrue once authorities recovered Ocera's body from its shallow grave in October 1991. After the body was exhumed, an arrest warrant issued for Leale, but the suspect never made it to trial: he was found shot to death in a Long Island parking lot four weeks later.

The Orena side eventually became convinced the case, like many others, was actually the work of Scarpa, the Grim Reaper, in his efforts to unseat Little Vic from the top spot and gain free rein to operate unfettered within the Colombos.

In court papers filed in 1997, attorneys for Vic Orena and Patty Amato argued that Scarpa and DeVecchio conspired on the Ocera hit in an effort to instigate the Colombo war. Judge Jack Weinstein described the assertion as "bizarre, but not entirely implausible," and Orena's son Andrew agreed.

"Whether it was Greg Scarpa, whatever it was that got Ocera killed, it was Colombo family business," he said of the killing. "It wasn't Vic Orena business. [Informant] Frankie Sparaco said it was John Gotti who did the hit. So maybe permission was given? Maybe it was set up by both families? I don't know.

"Did it come from John Gotti? Possible. But I don't think there's anybody left to dispute things, everyone's gone that was there. As far as my father, he said, 'Tommy's gone.' That's all he said."

The intrigue continued into the new millennium: a close friend of John Gotti Jr.'s would testify at the 2006 trial of the second-generation Gambino family boss that John Gotti Sr. set the war in motion in a power play to increase his control of the Mafia's ruling Commission.

"He figured if he could get Junior Persico out as boss and Vic Orena in, he would have another vote on the Commission," said witness Michael "Mikey Scars" DiLeonardo.

Andrew Orena recalled that Gotti, one of his father's backers, had little use for Persico—and vice versa.

"John Gotti and Carmine Persico hated each other with a passion," he recalled. "My father at that point had too many allies, which made him a threat to the FBI and the behind-the-scenes Persico faction."

Either way, the Ocera murder resonated across the Colombo family, for better and worse. Within a month of the killing, a redacted government document quoted a source as confirming that the "Gambino family is the one that authorized the Ocera hit, without permission of the hierarchy of the Colombo family."

It was yet another troubling reminder of the growing number of loudmouth mobsters now in the embrace of the FBI, openly sharing information with the feds.

According to the paperwork, "Gotti had Ocera killed because of a drug deal [marijuana]. Source advised that the members of the Colombo LCN family are very uneasy about the above hit. Source has advised that Carmine Persico has been sent a message, that he should name a permanent BOSS by January 1990 and if he does not, 'there will be trouble.'"

The reigning mob Commission, with Gigante, Gotti, and Lucchese head Vic Amuso, also expressed their support for Persico's son, Little Allie Boy, to take his father's seat upon finishing his latest stint behind bars, the document said. The Gotti mention seemed somewhat strange, given his friendship with Orena.

The single-page memo concluded with a prescient take on the rising storm within the family and the festering ill will among the Colombos.

"Source is of the opinion that Persico will not name a successor and open warfare will break out in the near future," the memo read.

As Orena retained his uneasy spot in the top seat, a heated family meeting where tempers flared led to Wild Bill Cutolo's demotion from his spot in the family hierarchy. Cutolo complained about the decision, declaring he had "earned his bones by having 'taken care of'" Orena predecessor Angelina, an FBI document recounted.

Carmine Sessa was bumped up as his replacement. John Orena recalled a conversation with his father when Little Vic was considering an earlier promotion for their colleague.

"Carmine was a very quiet guy, and I said to my father once, when he was thinking of making him consigliere, and I said Carmine's not that good of a talker," he recounted. "And he says, 'Yeah, but he's a good listener.'"

Sessa instead emerged as a divisive presence within the Colombos. There was an immediate problem: Sessa wanted to kill Cutolo, but Orena flatly rejected the proposed hit during a meeting in one of his sons' backyard. Little Vic's position was that the demotion was punishment enough.

"My father was adamant: nobody's going to kill Billy," said Andrew. "My father did the right thing by taking down Billy. But my father wasn't looking to take over the family."

The stress level inside the family peaked in the middle of June 1991, and the Orenas were unaware that the plot to murder Little Vic was already in the works.

"Carmine is acting a bit mysteriously at this time and it's a bit noticeable to us," recalled Andrew. "The quiet tension was so thick you could cut it with a knife. Those in my father's inner sanctum sensed that foreboding atmosphere, that things were changing.

"But we didn't know it would be the end of our glory days, before our descent into hardship and tragedy."

On June 14, 1991, Vic Orena took time on the day of his son Peter's wedding to address Sessa about conducting a poll of family members to determine the future of the Colombos under his leadership. The lingering dispute put a damper on what should have been a joyous day of celebration.

"The night of the wedding, the quiet tension was so thick you could slice it with a knife," recalled Andrew.

The Orena brothers insist to this day that the vote included all members of the family, not just the upper hierarchy, and that Little Vic carried the day with 70 percent of the participants despite a significant number of Persico backers and relatives.

According to John Orena, Carmine Sessa went directly to Scarpa after completing the poll, and the predictable and lethal war was set in motion as the messenger jumped ship to join the Grim Reaper's crew.

"Carmine was crying to Greg Scarpa, 'You know Vic's going to kill me!'" recalled John Orena. "And so who's Greg Scarpa? And he goes to the FBI."

Court documents later recounted that Orena had also asked Sessa to start bad-mouthing Persico by alleging that the jailed boss was a "rat" who should be "knocked down" as head of the Colombos.

But according to Andrew Orena, his father was content with things the way they were and had no intention of starting what became the last of the wars for control of the Colombos.

"My father would have never made a move on the Persicos," he said. "My father was loyal to them. He was running things, and things were going very well. And the Persicos, he didn't take any money from them. Now, my father, he's no angel, there's no wings on his back, but he would never have hurt the Persico family. Never.

"But the truth be told, the Colombo family needed a voice on the Commission. And it was really John Gotti pushing for my father to get a seat on the Commission. It was essential for him to be the boss."

The Orena brothers recalled the late Gotti as a larger-than-life figure, who was among the guests at Peter's wedding on that fateful day.

"He was as stand-up as can be and a tough guy," said Andrew Orena with a chuckle. "And he was a comical guy, a good sense of humor. He was a true outlaw, a James Cagney character. Listen, they wanted to kill him. Gaspipe and Amuso wanted to kill him. The Chin wanted to kill him. But they couldn't because he had twenty guys walking around with him every day!

"And they had the feds watching them 24/7."

The failed hit on Little Vic followed in short order once the votes were counted, and the divided family inexorably edged closer and closer to the inevitable war inside the Colombos. On the same night of the failed hit on Little Vic, in a particularly macabre touch, Andrew Orena recalled that his two older brothers were invited to dinner by Teddy Persico but begged off.

"I don't want to berate the Persico family; they've been through enough," said Andrew. "They're just like us, but they had been in that game a lot longer, and we were new to this on that level. But once that move was made on my father, that was it—that relationship, that tie, those things were gone."

No Surrender

The Colombo family combatants finally took to the streets of Brooklyn and suburban Long Island between late 1991 and 1993, pitting the two previously inseparable mob clans in a conflict destined to decimate both sides.

The first shots were fired by the Orena side at notorious Persico fighter Greg Scarpa. In a year during which New York City reported 2,571 murders, Mafia violence still made headlines for its lawless, shocking, and brutal nature that left bullet-riddled bodies on the city's streets.

The truth was impossible to deny: the two factions were fighting over a family on its last legs inside a business that had already seen its best days and had been under FBI scrutiny for years.

A 1984 FBI memo had actually laid out federal plans for a takedown of Colombo's leadership, starting with Carmine Persico and another ten captains, soldiers, and associates. The Colombos were first targeted in 1980 by operation Eclipse Star beginning, when court paper identified Persico as the boss.

The paperwork discussed the upcoming move to topple the operation: "The indictment will charge these individuals with operating a criminal enterprise known as the Colombo LCN family. . . . This indictment will be significant in its scope and effect on the existence of the Colombo LCN family."

The resulting arrests and convictions had opened the door for loyal Little Vic to emerge at the top of the family hierarchy. Orena was left to walk a fine line, hoping to operate as more than simply a placeholder for Persico's imprisoned son, while still pledging his fealty to the jailed boss.

"Vic's reputation was more a wealthy businessman than a mobster," said the FBI's Bruce Mouw. "He was well respected and not a person who liked to kill people. He's not one of those guys."

Things were about to change in the near future.

There was an early hint of the coming conflict. On January 14, 1987, fifty-six-year-old Salvatore Scarpa was gunned down inside a Brooklyn social club after five armed men burst inside just before midnight. The Grim Reaper's brother was killed by two shots to the chest and a third to the head, supposedly after refusing to surrender his property to the invading robbery crew.

But the victim's watch, along with a gold pendant and a wallet with $313 in cash, was recovered alongside his lifeless body. The alleged thieves had fled, oddly enough, without robbing their target. The *New York Times* reported that local and federal investigators were considering whether the killing was sparked by a fight for control of the Colombos following the Persico prosecution.

Carmine Persico had been sentenced only one day earlier, after his conviction in the Commission trial.

Years earlier, Salvatore Scarpa had offered a less-than-glowing take on the Mafia's future in a chat with an FBI agent. The elevator company worker and Colombo family veteran griped about the changing times; his view immortalized in an FBI document.

"Scarpa advised the 'old timers' are dying off, and that the kids coming along today are different and not interested in taking their place," the document read. "He stated to the agent that if this keeps up, the agent would be 'out of a job.' He refused to elaborate on this statement."

It took four years after Salvatore's murder for the Persico side to target Little Vic outside his home on that fateful night that ended Orena's efforts to keep the peace. During his meeting afterward with Teddy Persico, the acting boss said he was willing to forgive and forget the killers dispatched to take his life but worried his sons Vic Jr. and John would be killed if he stepped down.

"He said that nothing happened that could not be forgotten in time," Andrew recounted. "Teddy said my father should step down and declare Carmine Sessa the boss. My father said that can't happen now. He thought his sons and Billy Cutolo would be killed if he stepped down. So then came a deadlock."

There was no immediate response beyond the rejected olive branch from the Orena faction to the failed Long Island hit on Little Vic, and his loyalists bid their time for months as tensions increased on both sides. Andrew Orena recalled a message Persico sent from behind bars that pitched a plan for the Colombos to operate as a separate entity from the Commission. But another complication ensued: Little Vic had recently taken to disparaging his old friend and boss.

The Snake, Orena told family underlings, was a rat—actually echoing an allegation previously made by the shoot-from-the-hip John Gotti after Persico's admission at trial of the mob's existence, violating the long-standing mob code of omertá.

There were other strange goings-on with the jailed Persico. Shortly after his bizarre legal turn at the Commission trial, he discussed an appearance on the investigative television program *60 Minutes*. He backed out at the last minute, but his departure was captured on camera.

There were also reports of Junior sharing mob-related information with a reporter at the *New York Daily News* in a brazen violation of Mafia norms. Orena ally Gotti had also expressed his dislike of the venerable mob boss: "Carmine is losing his mind. [Persico] says this guy is nobody, this guy is nobody, this guy is nobody.... He is the only guy who's somebody."

The other New York families quickly gathered to establish a shaky truce between the two sides, one that went up in smoke and gunfire within a mere four months. The tension was soon unrelenting.

Little Al D'Arco later recalled the fruitless sessions during the summer of 1991 in which he and the heads of the Genovese and Gambino families tried to broker a peace after the failed hit on Orena. The Bonannos were excluded, he recalled, because powerful Genovese boss Chin Gigante was "deadly against them."

The Gambinos sent three representatives, including John Gotti Jr., and Chin's family dispatched three members as well. According to D'Arco, Orena refused to surrender his seat because the other side had kicked things in motion by targeting him. Additional attempts at reaching some sort of mob détente were equally doomed.

"We had a series of meetings," recounted D'Arco after cutting a deal with prosecutors to become a government witness in September 1991. "The purpose was to settle the dispute before the shooting began. We were going to tell them there is no shooting, no shooting each other."

Orena bluntly declared he would have stepped down as the family's acting boss if Persico had simply come to him with a request for his departure. But Little Vic dug in after the failed attempt on his life, opting for war over détente.

"They tried to clip me," complained Orena, who attended all the meetings.

The people behind the failed assassination plot showed no remorse, and the festering ill will from the other side continued to grow. Persico rep Carmine Sessa appeared separately to pledge his fealty to the imprisoned mobster and bailed out after attending a single meeting, a clear sign that peace was at best unlikely and that the divided sides were headed for a showdown.

Andrew Orena later recalled a second failed attempt on his father's life. One morning he had driven past Little Vic's safe house and spotted Sessa again sitting with other men inside a blue Lincoln Town Car before they sped away.

"I flew in the front door screaming 'Pop! Pop!'" he said. "He came running out of his room with a .380 Beretta, and he was screaming, 'What's wrong? Are you OK?' And I said, 'Carmine Sessa just pulled out of your block.'"

Father and son, with Vic slouching beneath a baseball cap, went out in search of the would-be hitters.

"That motherfucker!" Andrew recalled his father shouting. "Get in the car and drive! I'm gonna kill that cocksucker and end this war right now!"

Sessa mounted a third try in November 1991, in a plot to whack Orena, Scopo, and a Colombo family capo on the streets of Ozone Park. The targets were gone when the killers arrived from a Brooklyn diner. Scopo was given a pass after heading to a Gambino social club for a card game, and the killers worried about the collateral damage if any Gotti soldiers were accidentally clipped in the gunfire.

And John Orena recounted leaving a Queens dry cleaner after picking up his father's suits and spotting a car with potential assassins lying in wait. He and a fellow Orena backer frantically flagged down a cab to Kennedy Airport, where they mingled with masses until they felt it was safe.

"Every day I would wake up and the reality would hit me, that this could be the day my father was killed," said Andrew Orena. "He was the number one target of the Persicos. And by this point there were already murders, shooting attempts, close calls."

An August federal court document filed by prosecutors revealed the first failed hit on Orena, implicating Persico backer and Sessa crew member Robert Zambardi as one of the would-be killers. The paperwork made clear that the flow of information to the feds about the nascent dispute indicated that the mob's oath of omertá was not much of a thing anymore.

"Five confidential sources have informed agents of the FBI that members of the Colombo family close to Persico, and concerned that Orena wanted to take over complete control of the family, ordered Orena's murder," the court filing stated.

As negotiations continued, a half dozen incidents of gunfire were reported with no fatalities on either side of the festering dispute. The fragile peace between the divided factions would collapse before Thanksgiving.

"Certainly not the best course of action to go to war," said Franzese, looking back on the battle without a winner. "And Junior was a fighter. He knew a sit-down could go against him since he wasn't on the street, and nor was Allie. In his mind, war was the only solution."

When the Orenas made their first move, they aimed to cut off the head of the Persico-friendly opposition: Greg Scarpa. By the time of the war, their target was boasting of himself in a court filing as "the most powerful entity in the Colombo Family and an authoritative figure who bowed down to no one."

While the Orenas knew of Scarpa's fearsome reputation for violence, they and their colleagues in organized crime remained in the dark about his second job as a paid government informant.

And FBI agents likewise remained unaware of Lindley DeVecchio's unique arrangement with Scarpa, although several would become uneasy about the alliance between the two as the war raged.

The November 18, 1991, hit by the Orena faction served as a spectacular failure rather than as a death blow. The murderous Scarpa survived to emerge as the deadliest figure on either side, a bloodthirsty killer who gleefully celebrated his lethal efforts.

The stone killer was on the wrong side of the flying bullets when the first shots were fired, courtesy of Orena backer Cutolo, who was motivated to action after an FBI warning five days earlier that he was at the top of the Persico hit list.

Wild Bill quickly opted for a preemptive strike to start the hostilities and take out Persico's deadliest and merciless advocate.

The Grim Reaper was exiting his Brooklyn home, accompanied by three members of his crew, as the group prepared for a trip to his Wimpy Boys social club. Scarpa was joined by his girlfriend's daughter, Little Linda, who was carrying her infant son when they climbed into separate cars and backed out of the driveway onto a one-way street.

A waiting white truck appeared out of nowhere, pulling to a stop and blocking all oncoming traffic. Behind the vehicle, a half dozen shotgun-toting shooters in black ski masks emerged from a van and opened fire as Scarpa and the innocent civilians made a miraculous escape from the shocking hit attempt intended to eliminate the most dedicated and devastating Persico backer.

Scarpa quickly veered his vehicle onto the sidewalk and zipped away, while one of the plotters' vehicles was struck by multiple shots intended for the mobster. Years later, FBI documents laid the blame for the botched attempt on one of the would-be killers pulling the trigger too soon, alerting Scarpa to the impending hit. An informant revealed that the gunmen already suspected the Grim Reaper was funneling information to the feds.

Scarpa was infuriated by the attempt in which his kin nearly became collateral damage, flying into a rage after the botched hit before dialing up DeVecchio.

"He called me almost immediately and said he knew who did it," DeVecchio recalled of their blunt conversation. "And I told him, if you retaliate and start something, there's no free pass. I warned him 'my people will be looking for you.'

"I said I can't do anything for you, nor would I if I could. Any consequences are yours. And he said, 'Yeah.'"

FBI agent Favo recovered a license plate left behind from the truck. Years later, a cooperating witness recounted that Scarpa was provided with the plate's information by an unidentified source. Favo would later recall sharing the details with fellow agent DeVecchio.

In a written report a day later, DeVecchio cited a source— likely Scarpa himself—as noting that the murder try "would start a shooting war between the two factions."

As word of the failed hit spread, the fortunate Scarpa reached out to his Persico colleagues, and a meeting was quickly arranged at the Brooklyn home of Joseph Russo's grandmother.

A decision to retaliate was reached in an instant, with court testimony years later indicating that the Persico side was already well armed in anticipation of this moment. Their backers would continue attending regular meetings into the next year for updates on the war and plans for the family's future.

The Persicos' first target for payback was Orena backer Benny Aloi. But the shooters "just missed," authorities later said. The Grim Reaper's plans for a personal response by whacking shooter Cutolo were undermined by a Thanksgiving Day report in the

New York Post alleging that Scarpa was working as a government informant—a then shocking charge deemed implausible given his storied mob past but enough to put the war on a temporary hold.

The agent and the mob killer met soon afterward at Scarpa's home, court documents showed, with DeVecchio instructing two fellow feds to wait in the living room as the G-man and the gangster shared a forty-five-minute conversation billed as a routine chat inside his kitchen. While his colleagues couldn't hear what was happening, they later said that the FBI agent's written summary of the event—soon known as the "Kitchen 302"—seemed brief given the length of their discussion.

It was a meeting that would later be discussed at length inside a Brooklyn courtroom as a pivotal point in the looming battle for control of the Colombos and the subsequent prosecutions.

The conversation between the agent and the executioner was no rarity: the pair met or spoke at least every ten days during the long war.

"The bottom line was Greg Sr. was a homicidal maniac, with a killer crew," said Andrew Orena. "He enjoyed his freedom for all those years. People knew who he was, and he was left on the street. Carmine Sessa told us! And there was a lot more to Greg Scarpa. He was involved in a lot of things we may never find out about."

Vic's son insists the Scarpa plot was not approved by his dad but instead was concocted by Cutolo, who had been bumped from his spot in the family hierarchy position by Carmine Persico.

"He was considered too braggadocious," said Andrew of Cutolo. "Carmine [Persico] and Billy were both up my father's ass. Carmine wanted to kill Billy, and my father said no. But once Billy missed Greg, then we were an active opponent. They were trying to shoot everybody and anybody."

The failed Scarpa hit dramatically upped the ante in the coming war. If the attempted murder had succeeded, and the Grim Reaper had been removed from the equation for the Persicos, the conflict might have ended quickly. Scarpa instead survived to emerge as a man on a mission of murder and mayhem—the most lethal player on either side of the conflict, on the prowl for vengeance against the Orenas.

Authorities later said he was responsible for four of the war's murders and two other failed hit attempts, by far the most active combatant on either side, as befitting his storied life on both sides of the law.

Born to Run

Greg Scarpa Sr. was the Brooklyn-born son of Italian immigrants. His father was a hard-working man who paid the bills by hauling coal. Greg, born on May 8, 1928, wanted no part of the labor-intensive work, instead embracing the neighborhood's organized crime figures.

The young gangster with a perpetually homicidal streak became a made member of the Profaci family, later to become the Colombos, after pulling the trigger in a 1953 mob execution. He emerged as a good earner, eventually running his own crew inside the family.

Scarpa was a mob contemporary of little Vic Orena's, who was born six years later and became a fellow member of the same crime family. Like Vic, Scarpa brought his son, Greg Jr., into organized crime and hailed from the same outer borough—home to his infamous social club.

But Scarpa, unlike businessman Orena, had a fearsome reputation earned on the streets and beyond. There were rumblings over the decades that he worked as a snitch, too, an assertion often dismissed because no one believed the FBI would employ such a psychotic killer. By one count, his murders numbered more than fifty.

Despite their shared histories and positions in the Colombo family, Little Vic and Scarpa didn't move much in the same organized crime circles.

"My father wasn't close with Greg," recalled Andrew. "He thought Greg was a shady character, that there was something wrong with him. My father was close with Carmine Sessa, and they would talk about Greg—the man had mystique. He was a strange guy, a very violent guy."

Scarpa, a man both cagey and cruel, quickly emerged as the de facto head of the family's pro-Persico combatants in the absence of their locked-up leader. At the time of the war between the families, the relentless gangster was sixty-three years old and HIV positive after receiving tainted blood in a transfusion from a mob associate.

His health woes did nothing to slow Scarpa down once the Orena faction fired the war's first shots his way.

In his early days with the Colombos, Scarpa became known as a steady earner with multiple illegal income streams: drug dealing, loan-sharking, bookmaking, credit card fraud, and auto theft.

But his loyalties, despite a sworn allegiance to organized crime, would eventually extend far beyond the Brooklyn family to include the Federal Bureau of Investigation. The legendary gangster became a confidential informant for the feds, playing both sides for decades before his shocking twin allegiances were finally revealed.

"The guy thought he was James Bond," a Brooklyn prosecutor later marveled of Scarpa. "He told his kids he worked for the government."

Reams of federal documents offered the hard-to-imagine tale of Scarpa's surreptitious snooping on behalf of the FBI, an arrangement in which he earned kudos from the feds in a long-secret role dating back to the Kennedy administration.

FBI paperwork from the last millennium said the informant was paid on a sliding scale depending on "the quality of information" delivered, while another document from November 1, 1962, praised the deranged Scarpa as "emotionally stable and reliable. He has never furnished any information known to be false."

A June 1963 five-star review of Scarpa's work as a "Top Echelon Criminal Informant" echoed that assessment of the Grim Reaper's time working both sides of organized crime.

"CI has furnished extraordinary information of great value to the Criminal Intelligence Program and possesses a tremendous potential to fully penetrate the NY Italian underworld. . . . CI is (among) top echelon informants who are members of La Causa [*sic*] Nostra. CI continues to provide information regarding the Italian organization and the information is of such a caliber that it could only be obtained from an active member," read one rave review.

During his decades-long run as an FBI insider, he was behind bars only once: a thirty-day stint for bribing two cops in 1978, a stretch where he was briefly out of favor with the feds. But the whiff of something strange about Scarpa continued, wafting through his mob cohorts—even as the idea of his alliance with the FBI seemed implausible to his Colombo colleagues.

"I was stunned when I found out about Scarpa," said Michael Franzese, noting his old Colombo associate's frontline role in the war. "Greg was a different breed. But it was important for Junior [Persico] to have Greg remain loyal. He was strong and a good ally for the Persicos."

Not all the mob veteran's associates saw Scarpa in the same light. A December 11, 1974, FBI report quoted a source saying he "has hated Scarpa for many years and several years ago went to [boss] Joe Colombo and told Colombo that he strongly believed that Scarpa was an informant for the FBI."

The mob vet was, at the time, already into a second decade working for the feds, including being summoned two times to assist in resolving a pair of hate crimes in the Deep South. His terrifying efforts on behalf of the feds were eventually fictionalized in the 1988 movie *Mississippi Burning*.

The agents first reached out to the New York office with a request for Scarpa, officially Informant NY-3461, after the Ku Klux Klan kidnapped three civil rights activists in June 1964: two white Jewish New Yorkers, Michael Schwerner, twenty-four, and Andrew Goodman, twenty, and a black Mississippian, James Chaney, twenty-one.

The trio was working for the Congress of Racial Equality, a civil rights group looking into the torching of a Black church. They were almost immediately presumed dead—and they were dead.

The Klan had killed them and made their bodies disappear.

A massive search conducted by a frustrated FBI turned up no sign of the missing victims. The call went out for Scarpa. His girlfriend, Linda Schiro, accompanied the mobster on his trip and recounted how he winked at a group of eight or nine federal agents upon arriving at a local hotel. One of the law enforcers subsequently appeared in their room and handed Scarpa a gun.

The gangster solved the mystery in short order by kidnapping a local Klansman and ultimately breaking his will with an escalating amount of force.

Scarpa first put the gun to the man's head, only to hear a story that turned out to be bogus. The mobster returned a second time and placed the barrel in the local mayor's mouth and cocked the trigger, only to hear more misinformation.

Scarpa, at his third get-together with Klansman, threatened to castrate the reluctant man with a straight razor. The bodies were soon recovered. Once the job was done, another federal agent recovered the FBI's gun and handed Scarpa a wad of cash.

The Grim Reaper and Schiro left Mississippi for a vacation in Miami. Within seventy-two hours, the three decomposing bodies were uncovered by the FBI from where they had been buried seventeen feet below a remote earthen dam outside Philadelphia, Mississippi.

Two years later, the Mississippi G-men again brought Scarpa aboard as they investigated a Ku Klux Klan attack on the home of a Black man who had made his grocery store available to residents to pay their poll tax and cast their votes during an election in the deeply segregated South.

Klansmen set Vernon Dahmer's home on fire. Dahmer was killed by the flames, and his ten-year-old daughter suffered severe burns.

A local radio/television shop owner—Klan official Lawrence Byrd—received a visit from the New York gangster and an FBI agent, who gained entrance to his business by pretending to look for a TV set. As they carried the new purchase to their car, things changed quickly. Byrd was pistol-whipped and forced into the back seat of the car, then driven to a location where Scarpa brutally beat a confession out of the Klansman.

"He was never the same after that," a local prosecutor later said.

Two months later, Byrd signed a twenty-two-page confession and implicated seven of his Klan colleagues. The tale became part of Scarpa's fierce resume.

The feds and the felon parted ways in 1975. But Scarpa was resurrected five years later after his meeting with DeVecchio and the agent's pitch for the gangster to rejoin Team USA in his role as an inside informant.

"It wasn't the money as much as I think he liked being able to say 'I'm helping with the FBI,'" DeVecchio recalled decades later. "I think they all think, in the back of their head, if they have a problem, they can come to you and get out of it—you know, 'You help me, I help you.'

"But the first thing I told him was, 'You get in a jam, I can't help you out.'"

There were concerns about the fearsome Scarpa's allegiances, even among his mob associates. Court papers revealed that the family once held discussions about murdering Scarpa over suspicions of his work as an FBI source in the late 1980s.

Their worries disappeared as his body count went up. The Colombo hierarchy was unable to believe "that if he was being operated by law enforcement, the law enforcement officers would allow him to be involved in murders."

Andrew Orena described Scarpa as a "major asset" for the Colombo side with his ability to operate with impunity on the streets as the fighting raged on and on.

"They paid this guy for years, they let him get away with murders," he said. "If there was ever an inkling that Greg or any guys in the family were a rat, they're gone—right? Greg was given a pass."

13

Dancing in the Dark

Only days after the failed Scarpa hit, the Cutolo-led crew struck again. Persico backer Hank Smurra, fifty-two, was shot three times in the head while sitting alone in the front seat of his red 1989 Lincoln outside a Dunkin' Donuts in Sheepshead Bay.

Smurra, nicknamed "the Bounty Hunter," was gunned down by a ski-masked shooter through the passenger-side window of his ride; police found a .38-caliber revolver tucked beneath the front seat of his car after the execution. The dead man, a participant in the earlier failed murder try targeting Orena, was reportedly a loan shark and an operator of a Brooklyn card game.

The Persicos, already convinced Cutolo and his crew were behind the Scarpa murder attempt, had by now made Wild Bill's murder a priority. The first plot, to target Cutolo at his girlfriend's Staten Island home, fell apart when they arrived to find he was already gone.

Take two was set for Thanksgiving Day, with a plan to murder him outside the home of his girlfriend's mother in a heavily Hasidic Brooklyn neighborhood. The killers spent $600 to purchase black costumes in an effort to blend in with the local

Hasidic population, along with fake mustaches, beards, and facial hair to complete their disguises.

The plot was called off after the *Post* story raised fears among the would-be killers that the Grim Reaper "would tell the law" about the hit, court documents later revealed.

A third plot against Cutolo collapsed in June 1992. Persico acolytes had gathering stolen cars, machine guns, shotguns, bulletproof vests, and armor-piercing bullets as they once more plotted to whack the Orena loyalist. The meticulous scheme included test drives of the escape route from Staten Island.

Their vehicle, as it turned out, was bugged by FBI agents, who quickly arrested two of the would-be killers.

The Orenas remained on the offensive in the early street fighting. On November 29, Persico backer "Fat Larry" Sessa was targeted while strolling along a Brooklyn street. The four-hundred-pound gangster lumbered to safety inside the nearby car of a friend, who was hit by bullets in the shoulder and hand. The intended victim was a nephew of turncoat Carmine Sessa's.

The next blow in the war, somewhat befitting the sudden spasm of pointless internecine fighting, left the wrong man dead: retired Genovese family soldier Gaetano (Tommy) Amato was clipped in a drive-by shooting in which Joseph Tolino, a Colombo associate and nephew of family capo Nicky Grancio, was the intended target.

The murder of the seventy-eight-year-old was the work of Scarpa and Larry Mazza. The fortunate Tolino escaped with his life after taking a bullet to his left foot while the two stood together outside the Mother Cabrini Social Club in Bensonhurst.

Guests at Amato's funeral included a team of FBI agents with a camera and binoculars. The Persico side actually apologized to the Genovese leadership for the fatal faux pas. All bets were off by then as the war kicked into a higher gear.

On December 5, Persico soldier "Black Sam" Nastasi, seventy-nine, was playing cards inside his Brooklyn social club when he was gunned down. The killer blasted him five times in the chest and once in the head before fleeing the 1:00 a.m. execution. The reputed bookmaker was a Colombo family veteran. His girlfriend was treated and released at a nearby hospital after surviving a minor injury in the gunfire.

Nastasi was targeted by a lone shooter who marched inside the club with a .9mm handgun and sprayed eight gunshots before climbing inside a white car parked outside the Belvedere Social and Athletic Club to make his getaway.

On that same day, Colombo capo Salvatore Profaci—in a conversation captured on a bug inside a mob lawyer's office in Camden, New Jersey—expressed his support for the Orenas in their fight for control of the family.

"Victor Orena is a gentleman, beautiful person," the New Jersey mob veteran declared. "Very, very capable. Very, very qualified, level-headed. Carmine Persico's losing his mind. Carmine Persico is calling press conferences . . . He wants to go on *60 Minutes*, Barbara Walter's interview."

He offered another prescient opinion on the fighting: "My grandfather, when I was a little boy [told me] Salvatore, 'When strength and reason oppose each other, strength will win and reason becomes worthless.' Now we started shooting and where's it going to end?"

Few shared his opinion—or heeded his advice.

The city's looming holiday season was again interrupted one day later by one of the most stunning shootings, which targeted an unlucky Orena backer who was spotted hanging Christmas decorations outside his home.

The Grim Reaper had taken to cruising the Brooklyn streets in search of fresh targets in bars, social clubs, and the homes of Vic's loyalists. Mazza was behind the wheel, with Scarpa in the passenger's seat, when they spotted Vincent Fusaro innocently draping a holiday garland on the front door of his Brooklyn home.

Fusaro never had a chance to open his presents and was left dead after Scarpa blasted him with three shots from a rifle before disappearing into the Brooklyn streets.

"I love the smell of gunpowder," declared Scarpa after the execution, reveling in his lethal work. The satisfied shooter then sent the satanic code "666" to his consigliere, sharing the news of his latest kill in what became an unsettling ritual for the killer as the infighting raged on.

"The Fusaro killing was entirely unplanned," he would later declare. "I shot Fusaro and hit him with the first shot. It was just good luck."

The thirty-year-old victim, a relative of Cutolo's, lived inside the Bath Beach home with his mother and grandmother. The devastated pair were left to plan his funeral after his murder by the man now known among the Persico group as "General Schwarzkopf" for his wartime leadership.

"Guys were getting shot left and right," recalled DeVecchio. "We had surveillance teams out on the streets, picking up anything going on to prevent hits. So it was an interesting time, to say the least. It certainly got me in trouble."

The killing spree was by now front-page news, with a tabloid headline screaming "SILENT NIGHT, DEADLY NIGHT" alongside a photo of a police officer standing over the body.

But the defining moment of the war was yet to come: an innocent bagel shop worker was caught in the line of fire just seventeen days before Christmas 1991, a cold-blooded illustration of the ongoing insanity inside the warring Colombos.

The city's holiday season was just kicking into gear as Matteo Speranza made his way to work through the dark and empty Brooklyn streets shortly before sunrise on the morning of December 8.

The eighteen-year-old employee of the Wanna Bagel shop in Bay Ridge was doing his boss a favor after agreeing one night earlier to fill in for an absent colleague. The teen had started working inside the three-story red brick building only two months before when his mother secured her son the new job through the mom of a shop co-owner.

He arrived from Bensonhurst to start his shift, the last one the teen would ever work inside the business owned by two men with connections to the Colombo crime family and Carmine Persico.

Speranza had no idea of what had happened in the preceding hours. Armed Orena loyalists had gone in search of two Persico backers as payback for the Fusaro killing. The hit team became spooked by a black Lincoln spotted driving past their parked vehicle, and the initial plan—executing everyone inside the vehicle—was quickly scuttled.

But things ramped up quickly after the Orena acolytes returned to the home of fellow loyalist Louis (Bobo) Malpeso, who had received a phone call reporting that his twenty-year-old son had just been dropped off at Coney Island Hospital with a gunshot wound to the chest.

The victim declined to speak with cops when questioned about the shooting. But a misdirected plan for revenge was quickly put into motion. Malpeso was later accused of ordering loyalist Christopher Liberatore to "go kill in the guys in the bagel store," a reference to owners and Persico backers Anthony Ferrara and Frank Guerra.

Neither man was there, as it turned out, but Speranza was inside and working the last shift of his short life.

Liberatore reached out to his father, Anthony, and the father-and-son hit team headed through the sleepy Sunday morning streets of Brooklyn with the dad behind the wheel to exact their revenge on Bobo's behalf. The pair remained parked outside the store after spotting a customer inside. Following the customer's 9:22 a.m. departure, gun-toting Christopher Liberatore entered the store.

The quiet winter morning morphed into a horror show when the son walked beneath the yellow canopy and stepped inside the bagel shop. He asked the lone employee if either Ferrara or Guerra were around. Speranza, after asking why Liberatore wanted to see them, then made what the hyped-up killer interpreted as a reach for something under the counter.

Liberatore pulled his weapon and opened fire. Speranza was shot a half dozen times in the head and body in a shocking and headline-making mistaken-identity homicide. A young man in the wrong place at the worst time was caught in the cross fire of the ongoing war.

"I heard five gunshots, three in a row and then two more," recounted eyewitness Angelique Napolitano. "I got up and looked out my window, and I heard cars speeding down the avenue."

The killer and his dad drove home to cover up their tracks. The son took a shower, while Anthony Liberatore dumped their car on a Brooklyn street before breaking up the murder weapon and disposing of the gun. The father's wife was told to call and report the vehicle as stolen, court papers later revealed.

The father later returned to the vehicle with other co-conspirators to wipe it clean of fingerprints and tear out the ignition to create the appearance the car was stolen. They then moved the getaway car to a remote area of Canarsie following a meeting with Malpeso inside an outer-borough OTB office.

"An innocent victim," said one NYPD official of the victim. "He received a call at home the night before because the person who normally opened up the store couldn't be there."

Liberatore, testifying four years later after turning government witness, recounted the cold-blooded shooting of the helpless employee.

"I didn't know why he was leaning down, so I shot him," the killer recalled on the witness stand. "Four or five or six times. Then we dumped the car and laid low for a couple of days."

The Colombo war was again splashed across the front pages of the city tabloids, with outraged local officials vowing an end to the carnage.

"They have no more right to kill each other than they have to kill anyone else," said Brooklyn district attorney Joe Hynes after summoning forty-one organized crime figures on either side of the mob war to the courthouse within two weeks of the stunning murder.

Their appearance was a sight previously unseen in the annals of crime in New York or beyond. The mobsters drove up in their Cadillacs, some sporting fedoras and others dark sunglasses, after receiving their grand jury subpoenas in an organized crime cattle call.

The sweep drew national attention, with *NBC News* anchor Tom Brokaw providing details over video of the mob assembly on the nightly national news. The gangsters, greeted by a media horde of photographers and reporters, remained mute as they appeared one by one, each refusing to waive immunity from prosecution once led into a small screening room.

Each man spent roughly five minutes inside before departing. Little Vic was not called, although Billy Cutolo was summoned, one of the many high-ranking mob invitees.

The attendees included Bobo Malpeso, the man whose son was shot just a week before. Mob veteran Vincent Cassio casually smoked a cigarette as gangsters milled about inside the court building.

"We're using other law enforcement techniques to make sure they understand this is going to come to an end," the DA declared.

Defense attorney Charles Carnesi dismissed the whole episode as a law enforcement sideshow for the cameras.

"It seems to me, pure and simple, that it's an abuse of the system when a district attorney goes out for no other reason than to inconvenience them and to bring them into this public forum," he griped.

The mob tension only grew as an uneasy ceasefire and increased law enforcement attention followed the Speranza murder.

Andrew Orena recalled a night when brother John and an Orena backer known as "Frankie the Wheel" left their father's house carrying pistol-gripped shotguns. When the younger son closed the door, the sound of a loud gunshot rang out.

"My heart pounded out of my chest as I thought the worst," he said. "I ran out to see a smoke-filled car, with Frankie and my brother looking a bit in shock. John didn't realize he took the safety off the gun and it went off, blowing a hole in the floorboard. Once I knew they were fine, I started laughing hysterically."

Vic Orena marked Christmas Eve 1991 by moving his entire family, three generation's worth, to an armed hideout in suburban Montauk, Long Island. Andrew recalled dutifully packing up his wife and their twenty-two-month-old son as the Orenas waited for the threat to pass.

The uneasy ceasefire lasted one week into the New Year, when the Persico tracked down highly regarded Orena capo Grancio outside his social club—a devastating blow for his comrades in the war and to any hopes of keeping the peace.

Mazza and Scarpa were waiting with shotguns on January 7, 1992, when the two assassins spotted their target's recently purchased Toyota Land Cruiser in Gravesend. Grancio was sitting behind the wheel as he chatted through an open window with his nephew, Joe Tolino, in the middle of the afternoon, shortly after 3:00.

"This one's for Carmine!" shouted Scarpa as the pair opened fire. Tolino survived his second mob hit in just two months, and Grancio was gone in a burst of gunfire.

It would later emerge there were two surveillance teams on the Brooklyn streets on the day of the fatal attack: a task force of federal agents and police detectives and the mob hit team waiting inside a car with a bogus police light on the dashboard alongside a cup of coffee.

The eventual version of what happened laid the blame on DeVecchio, with allegations (and a lawsuit by the victim's family) asserting that the federal agent ordered his team to pull out, giving the killers a free pass to execute their rival.

Persico loyalist Mazza later recounted how Grancio pulled his vehicle over, perhaps believing they were law enforcement officers after seeing the bogus siren.

Mazza pulled the trigger of his shotgun from about six inches away, so close he could have reached out and touched the doomed Nicky Black. He pumped a load of shotgun pellets into Grancio's head, tearing the victim's nose torn completely in the barrage.

An FBI agent would later say his first suspicions of the alliance between the Grim Reaper and DeVecchio came shortly after the brutal execution.

The screams of Grancio's terrified nephew were audible to the killers as they drove away. Mazza recalled how he joined a fellow cold-blooded gangster afterward for a glass of wine as they watched an episode of *Seinfeld*.

The execution in broad daylight deeply rattled Nicky's colleagues inside the Orena faction, where the veteran gangster was held in high esteem.

"A sad day for us," recalled Andrew Orena. "On that day I was in the car with my father when Nicky called him on his cell. My father told Nicky, 'Go home, lock in, you're in the heart of Beirut.' Nicky assured my father not to worry. We went to my brother Vic's house and Pop settled in a chair and began to nap."

Word of the hit soon came from a pale and shaken John Orena, who shook his head sadly to Vic Jr. and then gently woke his dad with news from an Orena loyalist: Grancio was gone.

"Tears in all of our eyes," recalled Andrew. "Nicky was a bigger-than-life character. We were all upset, every one of us."

The execution targeted a mob veteran of decades with a lengthy resume: Grancio beat the rap in the 1975 murder of a Colombo associate whose body was found in the East River, stuffed inside a fifty-gallon drum. And he was a one-time vice president of a Teamsters local, reportedly serving as the family's man at Kennedy Airport.

"My father slumped into his chair, burdened by the divide in our family," said Andrew. "Guys that he loved within both factions, remembering what he told Teddy Persico before all the shooting started: 'No one wins in a war, the only one that will is the government.'

"How prophetic and true that became."

Mazza, years later while in the embrace of the FBI, recounted how Scarpa was frequently in touch with DeVecchio throughout the war.

"The way it was done, we would pull over to phone booths," he recalled. "We used cell phones and two-way radios to be in contact with DeVecchio. It was a constant back and forth. Scarpa would say, 'It's my girlfriend [on the phone],' and I knew who it was . . . and I knew what that meant."

Payback came quickly. Thirty-six-year-old Persico loyalist Steven Mancusi was shot three times outside his Staten Island home, miraculously surviving the hit attempt. But his good fortune soon expired: his decomposing and bullet-riddled corpse was discovered October 7, 1992, inside a car parked on a Brooklyn street.

The Persico crew had by then already struck back on March 25, when they executed Orena backer John Minerva and his friend, Michael Imbergamo, inside a champagne-colored Cadillac parked outside a coffee shop in Massapequa, Long Island. The two had just exited the Broadway Café, an Italian restaurant opened only three months earlier.

A pair of assassins opened fire, and the pair were struck by seven bullets before the hit team sped from the scene. The sixty-six-year-old Minerva was targeted after defecting to the Orena side of the war. The innocent Imbergamo—a plumbing inspector and Republican committeeman—was in the wrong place at the wrong time.

One of the lethal conspirators was capo Anthony Russo, a former Orena captain who flipped to back the Persicos. Court papers later revealed that the hit followed multiple meetings of the Persico faction in which Scarpa and Carmine Sessa griped that they were "unfairly shouldering the burden" in murdering Orena backers, prodding the Russo crew into action.

Minerva was specifically cited for death because he opted for Little Vic over the Persicos once the war began, the court papers said. His execution quelled complaints about the Russo crew's lethal efforts.

The execution came two weeks after an earlier attempted hit had failed, and Sessa congratulated Joseph Russo for his "nice work" in taking out the Orena backer.

The killers gathered afterward inside Wolf's Delicatessen in Manhattan to celebrate the twin slayings, with Russo noting a personal motive: Minerva had worked for years with his father before taking Little Vic's side in the fight. Russo would later argue, unsuccessfully, that Greg Scarpa was responsible for the executions.

Both of the victims were armed, but neither had a chance to pull their guns. Devastated family members at Imbergamo's funeral said he was killed simply for being in the wrong place at the wrong time. The Rev. Tom St. Pierre, in his eulogy for Minerva, recounted the killing and called for divine intervention in the war.

"Last week, a dark cloud settled over your family, this parish, and the community," he declared. "The violence, the blood, the shock, the evil, the horror, the ugliness, the cruelty that is sometimes is a part of life came to surface in front of the Broadway Café.

"We pray that all those who are thirsty for blood and vengeance may be thirsty instead for peace and forgiveness."

His prayers went for naught, too late to spare the victims. And Little Vic didn't know it yet, but his time on the streets was about to end as well.

On April Fool's Day of 1992, Orena was arrested inside his suburban Long Island "safe house" shortly after the sun rose by a legion of FBI agents—an event that failed to end the war or stop the bloodshed.

The future, once so bright for the Orenas, was darker than any of them could ever have imagined a mere four years earlier—and was getting worse, as they would learn.

Three months earlier, authorities had received approval to place bugs inside vehicles linked to the Orena faction, including Little Vic's, his namesake son's, and the boss's driver, Joseph Audino. The feds initially asked for a thirty-day usage of the bug and received a thirty-day extension as the targets spoke freely about the mob while the government recorded their damning chats.

In a bizarre turn of events, one of the bugged cars—a Pontiac Bonneville—was actually purchased from a car dealership run by Vic's son Andrew.

The Orenas and Audino routinely used an ever-changing number of automobiles during 1991, with Little Vic spotted by authorities in five different vehicles over a thirteen-month stretch as the wartime paranoia grew.

An informant told the FBI that Orena and Audino were partial to switching cars repeatedly over concerns of assassination, but the feds were nevertheless able to install the listening device inside the driver's main vehicle.

The recordings, federal authorities wrote in court papers, revealed Orena "in all his thuggish traits." The "Audino bug" intercepted conversations in the two months prior to Orena's arrest, offering a firsthand glimpse into the war-torn family's mindset.

The recordings showed three Orena hit teams were hunting for their mob foes while simultaneously pondering whether the Persicos were in turn coming for them.

"During one particular intercepted conversation, there was a discussion about weapons, watching out for 'the rebels' [presumably a reference to the Persico faction] and the safety of a particular [ally]," read one court document. "In another, the topics discussed included a shooting from a car and how 'Vic' had become the boss."

Audino was caught on one recording identifying three Orena "murder crews" by naming their captains: Vic Orena Jr., Cutolo, and Amato. A separate recording captured a chat about keeping their cars clean of anything incriminating: "They search the car. That's why you can't, ah, do nothing. You can't carry no shit. You wind up in the fucking can."

In a taped conversation on another listening device, Vic's son John offered an optimistic take on the family's future, declaring the Orenas were "starting to build up again" despite the ongoing war. And yet, in another intercepted chat sounding a telling note, law enforcement caught wind that Orena would surrender his position atop the Colombos if asked, bringing an end to the conflict.

It would have been an expensive decision for the acting boss: court documents alleged that Little Vic collected more than $1,000,000 from his loan-sharking business in three years, including $350,000 in 1991 alone.

There was more, of course: another intercepted chat caught the participants discussing weapons, with a warning to "watch out" for the Persico crew's loyalists and the safety of a particular location.

A Colombo family associate, in a bit of mob days from yore, was caught discussing the breaking of legs for those behind in their loan-sharking debts. The court document mentioning the strong-arm tactics included a recorded conversation in which son John Orena implicated his dad and brother in loan-sharking, including a $40,000 loan to an informant at an interest rate of 3 percent per week. Another informant reported collecting more than $1 million in interest from illegal loans during 1990 alone.

And there was mention of Little Vic's involvement in his namesake son's lucrative bootleg gasoline business.

The Orena side only discovered the bug when Audino returned to Andrew's dealership complaining of a gasoline smell inside his car. A service manager took a look inside to find the wiring setup under the vehicle's back seat.

"Looked like something out of a *Star Wars* movie," recalled Andrew. "A tracking device that led through the ceiling panel, attached to microphones, a whole elaborate system that clearly wasn't part of the original factory equipment. As soon as my brother Pete and I saw it, we simultaneously shouted 'Holy shit!' Within fifteen minutes, the dealership was surrounded by FBI agents with a warrant to seize Chubby's vehicle.

"We knew immediately this couldn't be a good thing for my father and my brothers."

14

I'm Going Down

Vic Orena's unwanted, if not totally unexpected, morning wake-up call from the FBI came as he was lying low inside the suburban Valley Stream, Long Island, home of his young girlfriend, Gina Reale—the daughter of an imprisoned Gambino family associate.

The fifty-eight-year-old Colombo boss was arrested and led away by federal agents on racketeering charges on April 1, 1992, after the raid on a spring morning gave the feds a clean sweep of the Five Families: the heads of each were now either behind bars or awaiting trial.

There was no sign of the coming storm in the hours before the law descended on the suburban hideaway. Orena's sons John and Andrew were both inside the Long Island residence on the spring morning, with Little Vic putting on a pot of coffee to start a new day on his last day of freedom.

"Get up, Sleeping Beauty!" he yelled at Andrew. "Coffee's ready!"

Orena sat chatting with John in the basement while the dead-end street outside quietly filled with carloads of FBI agents.

101

They were soon joined by Andrew, still in his underwear, around 9:30 a.m.

When the Orenas heard some banging from above, they assumed that workers painting the upstairs had just arrived to start their day's work. Vic Sr., with an abundance of caution, asked Andrew to take a peek through the door at the top of the basement stairs just to be safe. The son carried a shotgun in his hands as he crept up the steps.

He opened the door just a crack to see a man in a blue windbreaker. Across the jacket's back were three letters in white: FBI. Andrew knew what was coming next, and it happened in the blink of an eye.

"The agent shoved open the door, and then two agents were on top of me," he recalled. "One grabbed the barrel of the shotgun, the other put a gun to my head. An army of agents descending downstairs are yelling for my father. They arrested my father and kept me and John in the house for hours while they searched the place."

Vic Sr. was quickly cuffed and led away. The head of the Orena faction suddenly pulled off the street and away from his sons in the middle of the war.

Among those involved in the bust was silver-haired James Fox, special agent in charge of the FBI's New York office. Once inside, the high-ranking fed asked the suspects if there were any weapons in the house.

"I don't know," replied John. "It's not my house."

There was another federal agent on the scene, one who would become a surprising ally for John and Vic Jr. in the years ahead: Chris Favo.

Andrew and John were ordered to lie face down as the agents began scouring the house for evidence. They soon discovered a dozen firearms beneath the back porch, including four loaded shotguns and two assault rifles. A federal prosecutor later revealed that Orena was also in possession of a briefcase holding $55,000 in cash.

"An agent walked in with a green garbage bag," said Andrew. "He looked at me and John and said, 'Did you guys say there were no guns? Well, we just found this bag full of guns and you two are in a lot of trouble.'"

The sweep of the residence also uncovered a list of telephone toll numbers used to find addresses for Persico captain Joseph Russo and a friend of Carmine Persico's son, Teddy, with court documents alleging that Orena had ordered hits on both the mob capo and the younger Persico.

The fifty-seven-year-old Amato surrendered that same day. Authorities cited electronic surveillance and (of course) an informant for prompting his arrest as the legal noose tightened on the Orena faction. Both suspects were quickly charged and jailed for the Ocera murder, and Amato eventually won a legal battle to receive a severance from a trial alongside his boss.

Little Vic also faced charges of conspiracy to murder Persico backers during the war, along with loan-sharking, weapons possession, and racketeering conspiracy. It was a dark day for the Orenas, but the worst still awaited their jailed patriarch.

"The world of omertá is rapidly evaporating," said Brooklyn federal prosecutor Andrew Maloney, following the latest arrests in the law enforcement war against the New York mob. The upbeat prosecutor even joked that the flood of recent of Mafia turncoats was "breaking the budget of the Witness Protection Program."

Orena soon appeared before federal judge I. Leo Glasser for a Brooklyn detention hearing in which the acting boss was held without bail despite an offer from the defendant's family and friends to commit $2 million in assets to secure a federal bond for his release.

Little Vic's appeal for house arrest was turned down flat by Glasser, who described Orena as both a flight risk and a danger to the community after Assistant US Attorney George Stamboulidis recounted the haul of weapons recovered from the suburban Orena "safe house."

The defendant, said Glasser, was "the acting boss of a family that is involved in a terrible struggle . . . between Mr. Orena and Mr. [Carmine] Persico as to who will control the family."

The news was no better for Amato at his separate federal court appearance on the same charges, in which the defendant also entered a plea of innocent to all counts, including the gruesome death of Ocera, before he was led to a waiting jail cell.

The arrests did nothing to stop the fighting, and the war raged on with Orena behind bars, his trial looming as things inexorably became worse. And then worse again. When word of her husband's arrest reached the devout Joan Orena, the bad news was double-barreled: Vic was in federal custody. And he was cheating on her. Just as devastating, her sons knew all about the affair.

The federal backslapping for a job well done would disappear in 1995 when prosecutors in a case involving Orena's sons acknowledged that DeVecchio had earlier shared an address for the mob boss's girlfriend with Scarpa.

Once the smoke from the morning's events lifted, with Little Vic led away and the FBI now gone, Andrew recalled climbing into his car and turning on the radio for some relief—only to hear a recap of the morning's raid.

"I'll never forget the news flash: 'The FBI just arrested Victor "Little Vic" Orena, boss of the Colombo crime family,'" Andrew recalled. He put the car in drive and headed into an uncertain future for his own family and the crime family.

It was fifty-four years to the day since Little Vic's father died in front of his eyes.

One day later, in another sign of the changing times and a bad omen for Orena, Gambino family boss and Little Vic supporter Gotti was convicted in Brooklyn federal court of multiple racketeering charges. The Teflon Don was finally convicted and sentenced to die behind bars.

The arrests on federal RICO charges were now increasingly the norm around the crumbling Five Families and were largely fueled by the testimony of turncoat Mafia members in the embrace of their one-time law enforcement pursuers.

Two months later, if more proof of the new mob world order was needed, Lucchese family boss Vic Amuso was convicted of all fifty-four charges in his racketeering trial, including nine counts of murder. The anonymous Brooklyn jury needed just seven hours of deliberations to reach their verdict inside the hushed Brooklyn courtroom where Little Al D'Arco was joined as a star federal witness by fellow informant "Big Pete" Chiodo, who survived an assassination attempt before taking the witness stand.

Amuso, his chin up and his head cocked to one side, said nothing as his fate was determined. The reading of his convictions took a full twenty minutes, after which Amuso shook hands with his three defense attorneys and headed off to serve life in prison without parole.

He remained behind bars for more than thirty years, with his latest appeal for compassionate release rejected in 2023.

The upcoming Orena prosecution made new headlines only months later when a federal prosecutor told US district court judge Jack Weinstein at a September hearing about information that one of the esteemed jurist's family members was involved in a money-laundering real estate deal with Colombo family associates. The allegation, made by an unidentified government informant, was not taken seriously and was denied by Weinstein.

When defense attorneys pressed for the release of Amato and Orena under house arrest if they agreed to avoid the Mafia, prosecutors argued that their freedom could topple the peace treaty between the warring Colombo factions. In the end, neither defendant ever made it home.

Code of Silence

Vic Orena's prosecution kicked off a mere seven months later, with Assistant US Attorney Andrew Weissmann describing the defendant to jurors as the merciless overlord of the Colombo family, a man intent on keeping his tenuous position atop the mob faction at any cost—including murder.

There was little cause for optimism as the Orena family arrived at the federal courthouse for opening statements in the trial of their patriarch. Vic's five sons, dressed in suits and ties, exchanged pleasantries with prosecutors before taking the seats each would fill for the length of the prosecution.

Little Vic arrived for the day dressed in a suit delivered to his holding cell by his boys, who made sure he was properly dressed for the duration of the trial. Andrew recalled missing just one day of the prosecution, when he left during deliberations after the birth of his son.

"The government's case was a monstrous one," Andrew said decades later. "Seven cooperating witnesses. Numerous recovered firearms, guns found under the house of my pop's girlfriend. FBI tape recordings from cars and the home of a Persico faction member."

While the defendant was accused of a single homicide, for the killing of Ocera, the prosecutor laid blame directly on Orena for the bloody mob war that left the wounded and dead strewn across the city. Little Vic faced additional charges of racketeering and loan-sharking, and optimism was in short supply for his sons.

The Ocera killing was "an example of the lengths that man will go to, to protect his business: Don't skim money from me," the prosecutor declared in his opening statement to the jury. "If you do, you will get what Thomas Ocera got. This case is about ill-gotten gains, power. And about what Victor Orena will do to hang on to these things."

He detailed the vicious Ocera murder, with Weissmann alleging that Orena's deadly ire was sparked by the siphoning of family loan-sharking money by the victim—and by his own criminal interests. Gambino family boss John Gotti had also called for the victim's killing .

"Victor Orena, by killing him off, was also doing a favor for John Gotti" in hopes of landing the Dapper Don's support in the festering Colombo war, said Weissmann. And Gotti wanted Orena on the Commission as a swing vote, ensuring a majority for any mob business brought before the five crime families.

"Orena wanted to be the official boss," the federal prosecutor continued. "He started bad-mouthing Persico for talking to the press and because his lawyer had admitted at trial that there was a Mafia."

Andrew Orena still views the whole thing quite differently.

"They needed the war, and my father had to be convicted in order to make a bad guy in the war," said Andrew. "They made it Vic Orena's war against the Persicos. My father was never offered a plea. Why? Because they needed to make somebody pay. So he never got offered a deal, and never got offered to flip—not that my father would ever do that."

Defense attorney Gustave Newman, in his opening statement, ripped federal prosecutors for their reliance on mob informants in making their case. The feds had lined up two of their most devastating turncoats, ex-Gambino underboss Gravano and one-time acting Lucchese boss D'Arco, to testify against Orena in their new careers as star federal witnesses.

"These witnesses have committed almost every crime known to man, from A for arson to R for robbery and including M for murder," he declared. "Their motives are to save themselves from life in prison and to keep their ill-gotten gains from a life in crime. They have replaced their guns with their mouths."

A pair of prosecution witnesses soon took the stand, with co-conspirators Michael Maffatore and Harry Bonfiglio testifying to the garroting death of Ocera on say-so from the boss, with the latter again recalling Little Vic's direct order for the hit: "I want this thing taken care of." And he recounted the details of the murder plot, testifying that the hit was prompted by Ocera's alleged theft of shakedown money collected for the Colombos from a suburban garbage-carting business.

According to Bonfiglio, his partner in homicide, Leale, boasted that "Patty held him and I whacked him." Leale was later killed himself as the war raged on, reportedly to ensure his silence in the plot.

Vic Orena Jr. was eventually charged in late 1993 with the Leale murder, yet another legal blow for his reeling family. The authorities alleged that the mob boss's son gunned down the victim in broad daylight after a wild chase through a hotel lobby and into a parking garage. Leale was shot seven times, and witnesses described Vic Jr. leaping over furniture in pursuit of his target.

Another four flipping mobsters appeared as witnesses against Orena before the main event. The feds saved their two most prominent witnesses for last, starting with Sammy "the Bull" Gravano.

John Orena recalled Weinstein asking Gravano about his Brooklyn roots and the judge casually chatting up the mobster turned informant before he took the witness chair.

The admitted killer of nineteen was still a shiny new toy for prosecutors, testifying for only the third time since embracing his new role as a federal witness and future social media star. His first turn working for the feds came at trial only months earlier, and it helped convict his old boss Gotti. Gravano eventually putting three dozen gangsters behind bars (and later wound up there himself for running an ecstasy ring in Arizona in 2001).

Fellow informant Little Al D'Arco was a man with a storied mob past, his affiliation with the Lucchese family dating back to 1959. He had emerged as a reliable earner, making money in a variety of ways: hijacking, drug dealing, burglary, arson, armed robbery. And he served as acting family head before embracing his FBI handlers and taking the witness stand.

D'Arco recalled taking his induction oath to omertá inside a Bronx kitchen: "I should burn like this paper if I betray anyone in this room." His decided to turn informant after becoming convinced of his imminent death at the hands of his colleagues, and he testified against a dozen of them.

From the witness stand, the mob veteran identified Orena in the courtroom, pointing a finger at "the fellow in the brown suit." Defendant Orena showed no emotion as he rose from his seat and looked toward his old mob acquaintance.

Little Al recounted the failed 1991 efforts to broker a peace in the Colombo war, of the multiple sit-downs the leaders of the Lucchese, Gambino, and Genovese families arranged in hopes of preventing an escalation of hostilities. He again told of the point-less appearances by Orena and Carmine Sessa, testifying to Little Vic's offer to surrender the top spot if asked directly by Persico.

Orena instead, as D'Arco told the jurors, found himself under fire by the other side in the war. Carmine Sessa, in contrast, reiterated his fealty to the imprisoned Persico and to his side of the war.

The diminutive D'Arco, just five foot seven and wearing a dark double-breasted suit, testified from the witness stand that neither side in the deadly confrontation was moved by a threat from the mob's ruling Commission "to freeze them out" if the violence continued.

Little Al testified that Orena admitted to the Ocera killing at a 1989 meeting of the mob hierarchy.

"He said, 'We whacked Tommy Ocera,'" said D'Arco. Orena, he recalled, then gestured with his hand toward the ground, a sign that the victim was buried after the execution.

The witness never blinked when grilled in a lengthy cross-examination about his own criminal history. Asked by defense attorney Newman if he, indeed, murdered people in organized crime and had spent his adult life on the wrong side of the law, D'Arco shot back quickly.

"Part of my juvenile life, too," said the feisty old gangster before exiting the witness stand. D'Arco eventually testified at a dozen trials during his decade in the embrace of federal prosecutors before disappearing with his family into a new life in an unknown location.

The star prosecution witness soon followed D'Arco's appearance in court: Gravano, who had actually started his mob life as a member of the Colombo family before a dispute with another gangster lead to his relocation in the Gambinos.

Sammy the Bull opened with a bombshell: Vic Orena had once reached out to Gambino boss John Gotti and "asked if we could help him" by murdering Scarpa. And, Gravano testified, the proposal was initially approved by the Dapper Don.

"John gave me a contract to kill this Greg Scarpa," said Gravano, a fellow cold-blooded executioner who knew where the bodies were buried. "[Later,] John gave me the order to cancel it, because it wouldn't look good for [Orena] for us to do the work."

Gravano explained further that within the mob, "it would be a little bit of a disgrace" for a boss like Orena to farm out the killing to another family. Orena had suggested the murder could take place at a pool hall where Scarpa was known to hang out.

Gravano's testimony also confirmed Gotti's backing of Orena as a permanent replacement atop the Colombo family.

"John Gotti was behind Vic Orena," he testified, adding that the Gambino boss proposed that Little Vic bring his case for the job before the next meeting of the mob Commission—a get-together undermined before it could happen by the arrests of Gotti and other family bosses.

Gravano echoed D'Arco's tale of the peace talks, offering this take on the failed efforts: "They obviously lost control of it." But he confirmed that the Gambino, Genovese, and Lucchese bosses approved Little Vic as the official acting Colombo boss.

Newman questioned why Gravano's sit-down with the FBI did not come with any written reports or recordings of their conversations, unlike the mobster's cooperation in the prosecution of Gotti.

"That's their business," he replied. "I'm not an FBI agent."

Asked about his role inside the Gambinos, the witness cited his most notorious mob hit: "I think I played an important role from the day we shot Paul Castellano"—the boss famously murdered on a Midtown Manhattan street only days before Christmas 1985 on orders from Gotti.

Prosecutors also called on veteran FBI agent Lin DeVecchio for boilerplate testimony that went widely unnoticed amid the tumult caused by the two turncoat gangsters.

The defense argued that the guns found on the day of Orena's arrest were in fact planted by the Persico crew. An FBI analysis of the single fingerprint found on the bag showed no match with Orena—or anyone else on his side in the war. But the odds still remained stacked against him.

During a break in the trial, Andrew recalled, there was an unexpected and interesting incident when FBI agent Favo approached him for a chat unrelated to the ongoing prosecution.

"He noticed me praying the rosary," the mob scion recounted of the odd and unexpected exchange. "He asked if I attended Catholic school, that he did. Next day, on another break, I asked Chris if I could talk to him on the side.

"I handed him a set of rosary beads that my mom had brought back from Medjugorje. I told him, 'I'll tell you what. I'll pray for your family if you'll pray for mine.' And he took the beads."

Divine intervention would not come for some time. Favo became convinced there was something very wrong with the alliance between DeVecchio and Scarpa and went public with his concerns in a move crucial to Vic Orena's sons.

Federal prosecutor Gleeson delivered the government's closing argument, unleashing a devastating tale of the defendant's short reign atop the Colombo family as the war raged on. By the time he wrapped up, any hope inside the Orena camp had evaporated.

"John Gleeson, that day, the lightning bolts were coming out of his mouth," said Andrew. "I want to tell you this—he was amazing. We kinda liked him. He was a gentleman with us.

And the crazy thing was my father had a wonderful rapport with Gleeson."

The former federal prosecutor, fresh off his conviction of Gotti at the time, recalled how the Orena trial was a welcome change from dealing with the Dapper Don and the bluster of his defense lawyer Bruce Cutler.

"Acrimony and animosity," he recalled of the Gotti prosecution. "But Vic wasn't that way. It was, certainly compared to others, a pleasant experience for a mob trial. His attorney was Gus Newman, a revered gentleman. And Vic was all business, but he said 'Good morning' and 'Good night' each day, shaking hands before and after court started and ended."

Andrew Orena agreed: "Everything was cordial, even enjoyable. And then when the trial began, they got serious."

His father's fate was now in the hands of a dozen strangers, who headed back for their deliberations.

16

The Price You Pay

A ndrew Orena, in the relentless grip of a panic attack, took a seat on the bathroom floor inside the Brooklyn courthouse—his chest tight, his lungs desperate for air, his own rosary beads in his hands.

Prayers would not be enough just four days before Christmas of 1992.

Just down the hallway, Andrew's world teetered on the verge of complete ruin as the federal jury returned on its third day of deliberations with a decision in his father's trial.

The third of Vic Orena's five sons had already bolted past the court officers, leaving his siblings to hear the decision inside the crowded courtroom. He and a family relative found refuge, if not relief, on the cold tiles of a men's room down the hallway.

"My nerves are shot," recalled Andrew. "We're all overwhelmed, we're frazzled. And the jury verdict comes in. I'm in the courtroom and I tell my brothers, 'I can't do it. I can't do it. I'm going to the bathroom.' So they were like, 'Are you alright?' And I was, 'Yeah, yeah.' My cousin Michael followed me. I'm sitting on the floor, and I can't breathe."

The jurors' verdict was unanimous: Guilty on all nine counts. Guilty of racketeering, murder, loan-sharking, weapons possession—and guilty of leading a faction of the crime family in the bloody and ongoing war.

Little Vic, as he was led away in handcuffs, sent a silent message to his sons still inside the courtroom: he raised a hand to his jaw and touched his chest—we took one on the chin, but we're still strong. Love you all. His head still held high, Orena disappeared through a courtroom exit to the sobs of his family.

The bathroom door down the hallway from the courtroom swung open minutes later with a resonating thud. Andrew's older brother John, who followed his father and brother Vic Jr. into the Life, spoke with tears running down his face.

"We lost," he said simply. "All counts."

The next voice belonged to Vic Jr., cutting through the devastation with words that seemed to channel the now-doomed family patriarch: "Don't cry. Wipe your faces, wash your faces. We're going out there with our heads held high."

The boys' upbringing by the man convicted just minutes before demanded no less. Even in defeat, the Orenas would show no outward signs of weakness or the devastation each one felt. And neither would defense attorney Newman.

"I won't jump over the net and congratulate my adversaries," he said. "I'm disappointed. I'm a sore loser."

Vic Jr. led the way, and the rest of the family followed as they exited the courthouse. There were, indeed, no public tears. And each of Vic Orena's sons ran the gamut of media on Cadman Plaza, their stoic demeanors hiding their devastation.

The show of strength and unity would not stem the bad news ahead: Vic Jr. and John would soon face a combined seven indictments, including their own charges from the Colombo shooting war and other allegations fraught with the threat of their own long stints in prison.

Vic Sr. was facing almost certain death behind bars on his conviction. His arguments for release would fall on deaf years in the coming decades. And the Orena family, after a three-generation rise from Italian immigrants to the top of the New York Mafia, was left reeling without its patriarch.

The future was bleak. The options were few. And the alleged role of DeVecchio in the war remained a secret to all.

"The conviction—a 'holy shit!' moment," Andrew recalls. "Now you're talking about my father's life—done. I watched Goliath whip David's ass."

But even before that, as Andrew sat in the courtroom seat that he would later bolt, the mob scion had a feeling that something wasn't right, although it took a while for the son to get past the conviction and begin to wrap his head around exactly what had taken place.

"During my dad's trial, I learned much to help my brothers going forward," said Andrew. "You know how they say—now the rabbit's got the gun."

Andrew couldn't give his father freedom. But he would forever keep the faith, trying to deliver to his father two things in short supply at the federal penitentiary: Hope. And justice.

Brother Vic Jr. was caught by a recording device offering a different take on the prosecution and the prosecutor once the verdict was returned.

"We're going to keep fighting," he promised. "We can't stop fighting. This motherfucker [Gleeson] couldn't shine my father's shoes."

Two separate trials ensued for Amato and Persico captain Michael Sessa, with each convicted in separate prosecutions as the Colombo war wound down without them. All three defendants appeared together for a May 24, 1993, sentencing, where Weinstein hammered the three combatants with sentences of life without parole.

Little Vic was, in fact, slapped with life imprisonment for racketeering and racketeering conspiracy, a life sentence for the Ocera murder, and another life term for murder conspiracy tied to the war—plus more time on charges of carrying a firearm in relation to a violent crime and possession of a weapon by a convicted felon.

Underboss Amato was also sentenced to life, plus a concurrent life term for murder and forty years for two loan-sharking counts.

Sessa, found guilty of conspiring on murder plots during the mob infighting, was also convicted for the May 11, 1989, murder of drug-addled associate Anthony "Bird" Collucio, who was killed over fears he might cooperate with authorities if arrested. The hit order came from Sessa's brother, Carmine, who instructed shooters to dump the victim "in a drug-infested neighborhood, let everybody think that the drug dealers killed him," prosecutors had revealed.

When found guilty on eight counts, Sessa turned and glared at the jury before denouncing the turncoats who testified against him: "I can't believe youse believed those two rats."

On the day of Michael's sentencing, which would leave him behind bars despite decades of legal arguments for his freedom, his mother was left sobbing in the courtroom as her son was led away.

"No, no," wailed Jacqueline Sessa. "God, what have you done to me? You can't do this to my son. Oh my God, you have killed me."

Orena, even while facing his own imminent legal demise, displayed the characteristics that had made him the popular choice

Joseph Colombo shot in Columbus Circle, June 28, 1971.
Courtesy New York Daily News. *Photograph by Mel Finkelstein.*

Young Vic Orena on the beach.
Courtesy Orena family.

Little Vic on the right and Charles "Chuck" Tuzo, Genovese family tough guy and Orena's best friend, as well as the best man at his wedding. *Courtesy Orena family.*

le Vic Orena and wife Joan. *urtesy Orena family.*

Lucchese boss Vic Amuso, Orena faction member Bobby Gallagher, and Little Vic. *Courtesy* New York Daily News.

Aftermath of hit on Orena loyalist Nicky Grancio, January 7, 1992.
Courtesy New York Daily News. *Photograph by John Rocha.*

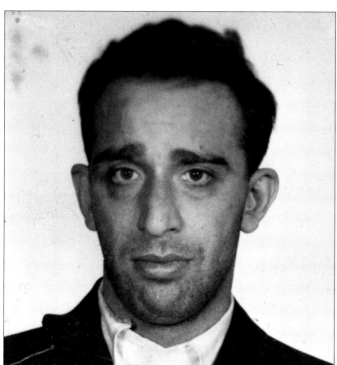

Carmine Persico's mugshot.
Courtesy New York Daily New

Greg Scarpa's mugshot.
Courtesy NYPD.

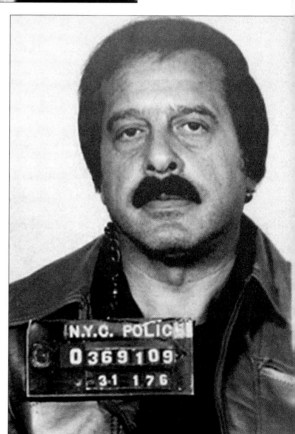

Vic Orena perp walk, April 1, 1992.
Courtesy New York Daily News. *Photograph by Jack Smith.*

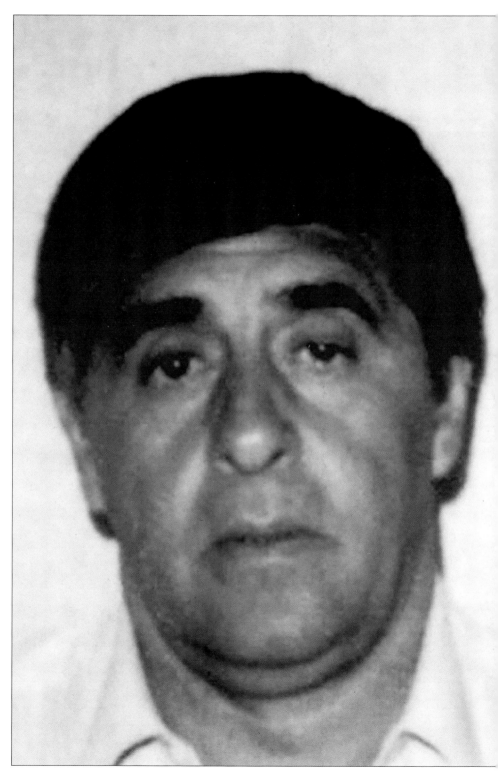

Little Vic's mugshot.
Courtesy NYPD.

among his mob colleagues for the position of boss. When Michael Sessa was facing his own 1992 trial, the Persico loyalist found himself running out of money as the case dragged toward its inevitable finish.

"You want to see how crazy this is?" Andrew asked now, a tone of disbelief in his voice decades later. "Michael goes to trial first. He don't have enough money. He asks the Persicos to help him with the lawyer, and they never give him money. The mother asked for money for the wife.

"My father was at the Metropolitan Correctional Center, and we told him, and he said 'give them $5,000.' And the Persicos wouldn't help him."

The evidence against the three men from their roles in the war exposed the defendants as "cold-blooded murderers and a great danger to the community," said sentencing judge Weinstein. "[The evidence] proves beyond any doubt that these defendants will not abandon their criminal activities and mob membership upon release from prison."

In addition, Orena was whacked with a $2.25 million fine, Sessa was ordered to pay $2 million, and Amato, $1.75 million. Weinstein, in a final flourish, ordered all three to pay the government a monthly $1,492 per month to cover their imprisonment costs.

The judge said the draconian prison terms were intended to steer others from the allure of organized crime.

"I believe there is a large part of the young Italo-American community that should be discouraged from going into this line of work," said the venerable Weinstein. "There is no need for it. . . . Young, impressionable males in the Italian-American community are lured into the destructive life of these mobs before they are able to recognize better opportunities."

For Andrew Orena and his brothers, nothing was the same once the verdict came in against Little Vic, which was then followed by the sentence that ensured their patriarch was never coming home.

"After my father got pinched and convicted, the world changed," he said. "All the loyalty started moving around, and it was disgusting to my brothers and me. How everybody was vying for his position."

In hindsight, said Andrew, his father's ascent was tied to the lack of qualified mobsters capable of running the family after Carmine Persico was convicted.

"The Persicos had no one they really could trust who was capable," he said. "My father was the most honorable among all of them, and it's ironic how things turned out. My father cared for the Persico family. He felt an obligation to look out for them."

There were more trials ahead for the Orenas and combatants on both sides. Soon all turned their attention to the role played by DeVecchio in the war, while defense attorneys kept digging into the details of the family bloodletting.

"Things unraveled in a hurry," said Gleeson decades after federal prosecutors jailed mob bosses Gotti, Amuso, and Orena in a single calendar year. "Scarpa, DeVecchio—how many significant things happened."

We Take Care of Our Own

R. Lindley DeVecchio, the son of a decorated army colonel, who was buried in Arlington National Cemetery, was born in Fresno, California, but found his life's calling three thousand miles east from there as an FBI agent working in the organized crime division in New York City.

The dapper DeVecchio joined the federal agency during the reign of J. Edgar Hoover, where he earned a stellar reputation among his federal colleagues after reporting as an FBI agent in March 1966, following fifteen weeks of training.

He was welcomed aboard with his classmates by a handshake from Hoover and assigned to the FBI office in Albany, New York, to pursue his hopes of a career as a crime-buster.

Just over a year later, on his birthday, DeVecchio was assigned to the New York office to investigate organized crime—a dream come true. He became the youngest agent ever assigned to the detail.

"To this day, I can't imagine a better job, a more fun job," he recalled. "I loved every minute of it. It was not my choice; it was by chance. I went to the OC squad and that was it. I got lucky. I liked it so much, I never left."

The OC agents were assigned to develop mob informants. DeVecchio recalled how quickly he took to the task, lining up a half dozen moles inside the Colombo, Lucchese, and Genovese families. While going through old case files, he came across the name of Scarpa, whose own paperwork revealed he was closed by the FBI five years earlier, after a long association with law enforcement.

In 1980, the now-veteran fed sought out Scarpa to successfully reopen the mobster. Three years later DeVecchio was promoted to supervisor of the FBI's Colombo and Bonanno unit and emerged as a key figure in the efforts to dismantle the five New York families, a mission accomplished as the feds eventually put the city's Mafia bosses behind bars in a series of high-profile prosecutions.

He recounted the first and fateful meeting with the Grim Reaper, a cold call to the cold-blooded killer on a sunny day in June.

"I literally drove to his house," he said. "I thought 'What do I have to lose? He's gonna tell me to go to hell?' He came out of the house and got into his black Lincoln, and I pulled behind him and blocked the driveway. And he said, 'Who the fuck are you and what the fuck do you want?' And I thought, that's a good start."

The initial response from Scarpa was a hard no, followed by a glimmer of hope: he took the agent's number and said he would consider the offer. Two weeks later, Scarpa called back and returned to his surreptitious work as a "Top Echelon" informant, quickly identifying Carmine Persico as the Colombo boss and naming five family capos.

"We set up a meet and he told me to come by the house," the agent recounted. "And he was my informant until 1992."

It was the agent's longest-running association with any of his moles. And this one would come with a ton of baggage as their relationship went forward and allegations began flying about their too-close ties and as Scarpa remained on the streets during the war.

DeVecchio had become widely acclaimed as a handler of mob cooperators, eventually instructing FBI recruits at the federal training academy in Quantico, Virginia, on the nuances of bringing informants into the fold—although his efforts didn't always pay off.

DeVecchio recalled a trip to Greenwich Village, where he crossed paths with Genovese boss Vincent Gigante at the mobster's Triangle Social Club. The Chin was already well into his performance artist phase, feigning mental illness to avoid prosecution in what became a long-running show on neighborhood streets as he shuffled about in a ratty bathrobe outside the apartment he shared with his Italian immigrant mother.

"Myself and an old partner went to talk with Gigante," he recalled. "Anyway, we waited a ways back to see what was going on and we see him, animated and talking to some guys. Then we got up to the front door of his social club and they stopped us, and we said, 'We want to speak with Mr. Gigante.'

"One of the guys had his hands up and touched me, and I said, 'Don't ever fucking do that again.' But we got to see Gigante fall into his crazy act. We could hardly contain ourselves from laughing."

In 1983, DeVecchio was bumped up to supervisor of the FBI's Colombo and Bonanno squad. He was dressed for the part, sporting a gold bracelet, monogrammed shirt, and a silk pocket square. And his ties to Scarpa strengthened over time, with the snitch referring to DeVecchio as "Mr. Dello" or the "girlfriend" in their phone conversations.

The federal agent ultimately emerged as a lightning rod for criticism over their alliance, including allegations that he was as much a criminal as a crime-buster for keeping the mobster Scarpa out of jail and in the loop about developments during the war.

But DeVecchio remains adamant that the two shared a strictly business relationship, despite all that happened regarding their ties. And he describes the fellow agents who later raised questions about his lengthy association with Scarpa as too inexperienced to understand what was going on.

"You're walking a fine line when you're dealing with criminals," he said. "Giving out addresses? That never happened. Pure bullshit. To some degree, [other agents] were new to the game. They didn't know about organized crime and how they operate. Scarpa was a hit guy for Persico, and everybody knew it.

"But it's one thing to know it and another thing to prove it. I was accused endlessly, 'How did you know he's a killer?' But everyone had to kill to become a member."

He also recalled an incident in which Scarpa's daughter, known as Little Linda, was reportedly molested by a man hired to drive the girl to school each day. The driver turned up dead on a Brooklyn street, with Scarpa the likely suspect.

"I asked him if he knew anything about it and he smiled," said DeVecchio. "He looked at me and smiled. I knew he did it, goddamn good and well. Why not report that? Because he smiled? Let's not be silly about this. What evidence? Any witnesses? An unsolved case."

By the mid-1980s, with the war still three years off, Greg Scarpa was facing legal and health issues. He was HIV-positive as the result of a 1986 blood transfusion from an associate when hospitalized with bleeding ulcers; Scarpa, refusing to get blood from a stranger, had issued a call for help from family and friends.

One volunteer was a weight lifter pal, who was already HIV-positive after using a dirty needle to inject steroids. The donor would die six months later, and the once imposing 225-pound Scarpa would lose 75 pounds in the next few years after becoming infected.

One year earlier, Scarpa had been arrested for purchasing three hundred blank Visas and Mastercards from an undercover agent. His case was resolved with a $10,000 fine and five years of probation after DeVecchio stood up for his informant, joining Scarpa for a meeting with the trial judge. Prosecutors had initially sought jail time, citing Scarpa's long criminal history and violent behavior.

Once the war began, the duplicitous Scarpa's ties to the agent remained hidden from combatants on both sides of the shootout. This was not his first rodeo, and Scarpa—by then more than a decade into his work as DeVecchio's star informant—emerged as the war's deadliest participant.

But the too-cozy interactions between the gangster and his veteran handler set off alarms for fellow law enforcer Favo, a senior field agent working alongside DeVecchio during the mob fighting. DeVecchio, in a memoir written years later, derisively referred to Favo and the other less experienced agents as the FNGs: fucking new guys.

"They were new to the game and didn't know about organized crime and how they operate," DeVecchio said in a recent interview. "In law enforcement, you bend a little to get good results, but you don't break the law. That's something a lot of people have difficulty grasping: 'You actually talk to people killing other people?'

"The realities are, as I said in the book, you don't go to the local rabbi or priest. You go directly to the source."

18

The Ties That Bind

Scarpa was closed as a federal informant on March 3, 1992, amid rumblings he was plotting another hit against the Orena faction: the FBI cited "credible allegations that Scarpa was involved in planning violent criminal activity."

But he returned on April 8, one week after Little Vic's arrest, after DeVecchio argued that the information about the Grim Reaper was the result of "mob paranoia" sparked by the conflict. The federal agent never told his supervisor about his move, which did not require approval from the boss.

"DeVecchio single-handedly reopened Scarpa as an informant," court papers revealed of their renewed collaboration. The lethal mobster reemerged front and center after barely a month back in the embrace of his FBI handler.

Orena backer Lorenzo Lampasi, sixty-six, was a survivor of the two earlier Colombo wars, going back to the days when the Gallo and Profaci crews waged a battle for control of the family. In 1974, Lampasi was seriously wounded only days before Christmas by a ski-masked gunman inside a Brooklyn hair salon.

His luck evaporated in the early morning darkness of May 22, 1992, when the mob veteran was gunned down while opening the gate to leave his apartment building parking lot.

Lampasi had just exited his 1988 Cadillac outside his Borough Park residence when the killers opened fire, hitting their target multiple times in the head and chest. Scarpa, accompanied by two fellow Persico loyalists, fired first from a car window before climbing out to pump a few more bullets into the victim.

"What did I do?" the dying man, shot nine times, asked with his final breath in the murder that changed everything in the ongoing battle of mob factions—and inside the FBI.

When word of the assassination reached DeVecchio, his oft-quoted response about winning the war left his fellow feds slack-jawed. The remark particularly rankled Favo, who responded that they were FBI agents and "not on either side of the Colombo war."

Court papers filed fourteen years later described another meeting between DeVecchio and Scarpa inside the killer's home, with the federal agent allegedly providing the target's address and a tip that Lampasi left home every day for work at 4:00 a.m.

Five hours after the Lampasi hit, Orena backer Richard Capichano, fifty, was shot twice in his left shoulder while leaving a Bensonhurst grocery store with a newly purchased pack of cigarettes. The wounded jewelry store owner climbed inside his car and drove ten blocks to Victory Memorial Hospital, where he was treated and released.

While the violence slowed, the pressure from law enforcement continued: within a month four fugitive Colombo combatants were busted inside a Jersey Shore apartment. But as the conflict dragged into the summer, DeVecchio raised more eyebrows among his FBI colleagues by telling Favo to stop making arrests without his approval, citing an overload of paperwork.

"I've had it!" he declared at one point in the summer of 1992, his voice rising in a forceful declaration. "You will not arrest another single individual without my specific approval!"

FBI agent Howard Ledbetter was taken aback by the outburst, as squad members did not typically need DeVecchio's go-ahead before taking suspects into custody. He would eventually come to believe "that it was possible that SSA DeVecchio was attempting to interfere with or otherwise stall the development of the investigation as it related to Gregory Scarpa."

For those combatants who didn't have a friend in the feds, the arrests continued: on April 8, 1993, the feds descended on the venerable St. Patrick's Cathedral, where prayers were not enough to spare fugitive consigliere Carmine Sessa or his mob colleagues. Sessa, Carmine Persico's brother, Teddy, and fellow Colombo capo Frank Sparaco were taken into custody on charges for conspiring to murder their enemies in the Orena camp.

The Palm Sunday arrests outside the Manhattan landmark ended a months-long hunt for the fugitive Sessa, who needed all of ten minutes to pledge his fealty to the feds, flipping to enroll in witness protection and eventually testifying in eight mob-related trials against his cohorts.

"Chris Favo had a good source," recalled FBI agent Jeff Carrie about the genesis of the arrests. "We picked up on a capo from the family, early on a Sunday morning. We covertly surveilled him into the city, to the meeting point at the cathedral.

"There was a guy driving a taxi with a fare in the back, and they were actually agents. Carmine Sessa was later quoted as saying he thought he was going to get whacked."

Mob chronicler Jerry Capeci, of the *Daily News*, noted that Sessa's rapid ascension through the ranks was not a good thing for the Colombos. Sessa was inducted in 1987, bumped to capo a year later, and elevated to consigliere by Orena.

"[His] meteoric rise . . . illustrates the talent shortage for top executives in today's mob," he wrote. "It is akin to an assembly worker becoming chief operating officer in three years.

"And like any corporation that doesn't take the time to train its top managers, the mob is losing its market share, as Sessa and dozens of other defectors leave the Mafia gasping for life and new leaders."

By July the two sides had declared a truce in the killing. And by the end of 1992, seventeen Colombo combatants were convicted of murder or conspiracy to murder, and another five on gun charges based on details provided by their fellow made men turned informants.

Though the steady drumbeat of the pointless war had ceased, the final shots of the conflict were yet to come—along with the end of Scarpa's free rein on the Brooklyn streets.

19

Ghosts

Scarpa's decades-long aura of invincibility took its first hit with a March 1992 warrant issued for his arrest on a weapons possession charge for tossing a loaded handgun from the window of his car. The mobster did not surrender or reach out to the Brooklyn district attorney but instead disappeared and contacted DeVecchio. The two subsequently met or spoke by phone while Scarpa remained on the street, authorities later said.

The Grim Reaper was in fact free to murder Lampasi before resurfacing five months later to testify in a malpractice lawsuit against the Brooklyn hospital where he had contracted AIDS, winning a $300,000 settlement that came with a cost: Scarpa was back on law enforcement's radar.

"Money has never been the issue," said a happy Scarpa while hugging his girlfriend, Linda Schiro, after his legal windfall. "My only concern was to put across to the general public about the kind of safety measures that should have been followed. Hopefully there won't be others who have to go through what I have had to go through."

His joy was short lived. On the morning of August 31, 1992, only two days after his legal windfall, Scarpa was arrested and booked on murder conspiracy charges tied to the Colombo war. The unrepentant mobster was held under house arrest and ordered to wear an electronic ankle bracelet allowing authorities to track his whereabouts while awaiting trial.

Four months later, the beeper on the bracelet went off.

Scarpa, enraged to learn that his son, Joseph, was treated disrespectfully during a drug deal, climbed from his bed shortly after midnight on December 29 to trade gunshots outside his Bay Ridge home with two men involved in the dispute. Scarpa, his left eye shot out by a bullet during the firefight, walked back inside his home and grabbed a towel to stanch the bleeding.

He then knocked back a glass of Scotch and climbed into his bullet-ridden car. He drove twenty miles to a Manhattan hospital for treatment, without notifying the police. Authorities recovered twenty-five shell casings on the street. Scarpa's targets declined to share with authorities any details of what happened.

Federal officials moved quickly to incarcerate Scarpa following the shootout. The senior citizen gangster was later relocated from a jail cell to a hospital bed after Judge Weinstein received proof from prison officials that the mobster's health had "seriously deteriorated" inside the Metropolitan Correctional Center.

Court papers revealed that the HIV-positive Scarpa's lifespan was down to mere months from the AIDS virus that was ravaging his body. The mobster had dropped another twenty-five pounds from his already gaunt frame and was suffering from bouts of dementia.

But, as Weinstein wrote in a March 5, 1993, decision to keep Scarpa behind bars, the "defendant's dangerousness must be taken into account. There is no doubt that this defendant, in spite of his faltering health, would likely engage in further criminal activity if allowed to go free."

The ailing Scarpa appeared to be on his last legs when he entered his May 1993 guilty plea on racketeering charges from the war, admitting to his role in the murders of Orena faction backers Fusaro, Grancio, and Lampasi.

On December 16, 1993, Weinstein erred on the side of compassion in sentencing Scarpa to ten years in prison, declaring that the reduced term would allow the murderous mobster access to a prison hospital rather than leaving him to die behind bars.

"Despite the defendant's dreadful murderous conduct and that of his gang, he is a person," said the judge, crediting his decision to a higher power. "While he has done acts worse than those of a wild animal, we would forfeit part of our God-given humanity were we to ignore his status as a fellow human being."

Scarpa made a last-ditch plea for leniency, the merciless killer now appealing for mercy.

"I expect to go home . . . I tried to help, your honor, I am sure you're aware of that," he told Weinstein. "I thought there was the possibility of me getting to go home."

Weinstein offered a terse rebuke to his suggestion: "That's impossible."

Greg Scarpa Sr. died on June 4, 1994, inside the Federal Medical Center in Rochester, Minnesota, a thousand miles away from the streets of Brooklyn.

"Bottom line was Greg Sr. was a homicidal maniac," said Andrew Orena. "He enjoyed his freedom for all those years. And people knew he was left on the street by the FBI."

Linda Schiro, speaking to an FBI agent three months later, recalled Scarpa asking her two years earlier to reach out to DeVecchio about his legal problems, to no avail.

"At Scarpa's request, [she] asked SSA DeVecchio if he could help [Scarpa] get released under a 'house arrest,'" said an FBI document. "Schiro remembers SSA DeVecchio told her that he could do nothing with respect to this request."

According to DeVecchio, prosecutors had tried to squeeze the ailing Scarpa for details on their relationship as the old mob killer angled to arrange for his death at home.

"And Scarpa said, 'No, DeVecchio never gave me any information,'" he recalled. "He was stand-up, God bless him."

20

Last Man Standing

The peace between the two sides was shattered barely a year after Scarpa's arrest and imprisonment when longtime Orena loyalist and underboss Joseph Scopo was executed in a hail of gunfire outside his Queens home on October 20, 1993.

The victim sat helplessly in the front passenger seat of his Nissan Altima when a failed run for his life ended in a hail of two dozen bullets.

The forty-seven-year-old victim, as it turned out, was allegedly killed on orders of Persico's nephew, "Skinny Teddy," who reportedly called for the hit while temporarily furloughed from jail to attend his grandmother's wake and funeral.

The mobster, after praying before her casket, took a seat in the chapel with three Colombo associates and signed off on the murder of Scopo, according to testimony from former family member Anthony Russo.

Teddy Persico, it was later revealed, was convinced the killing would end the war, which up until that night had already ceased for months.

Scopo was gunned down after returning from dinner with his nephew and future son-in-law. The death of the family underboss became the final murder in the war, with the victim gunned down even as both sides were already facing a series of prosecutions brought with the help of their turncoat colleagues.

Scopo was targeted inside the tan-and-gold 1993 vehicle driven by Angelo Barrone, twenty-seven, with nephew Dominic Logazzo, twenty-six, riding in the back seat. When the trio arrived at Scopo's home in Ozone Park around 11:00 p.m., the assassins emerged wielding a MAC-10 automatic pistol and a .380 automatic pistol.

Scopo immediately bolted from the parked car and ran for his life, making it two doors down before he was mortally wounded by three of the flying bullets. Cops later said that roughly thirty rounds were fired and twenty-three shell casings recovered. Scopo's innocent nephew took a bullet to the arm.

"I am very much concerned that this killing might mark a renewal of warfare within the Colombo family," said Queens district attorney Richard A. Brown.

Scopo was the former vice president of Local 6A of the Cement and Concrete Workers Union in New York City and the son of Colombo family bigwig Ralph Scopo Sr., who died behind bars while serving a one-hundred-year jail term for racketeering following the federal Commission trial, alongside Carmine Persico.

"I heard shots," recounted neighbor Bob Tobasco, a UPS driver. "It sounded like a pack of firecrackers going off. There were four or five shots. I assumed it was an Uzi rapid-fire or a machine gun of some kind. I saw a guy lying on the ground. I was just holding his hand, trying to comfort him a little. When his son came out, he snapped out of it. He snapped out of it as soon as he saw his son's face."

Scopo died two days later at Jamaica Hospital. The shooters fled in a stolen car, which was later recovered with a weapon and a silencer left behind by the assassins. A full two decades later, Persico faction associate Big Frank Guerra—one of the intended targets in the botched the bagel shop murder—was identified as one of the shooters after his conviction as a drug peddler.

According to federal officials, in addition to the Scopo murder, Guerra was responsible for the 1992 execution of Michael Devine, a victim with no mob ties beyond his romance with Little Allie Boy Persico's wife while her husband remained behind bars.

The killer, authorities later alleged, made sure to fire two bullets into Devine's crotch. Guerra was initially cleared at trial after witnesses testified that the gangster was at home with Colonel Mustard and Professor Plum, playing a game of *Clue* on the night of Scopo's execution.

His good fortune didn't last.

In September 2013, Guerra was sentenced to fourteen years in jail on the drug charge, with a press release declaring a "preponderance of the evidence [showed] that the defendant had committed numerous additional crimes," including the two hits.

With the fighting now over, court papers detailed how the FBI intervened repeatedly during the war to slow the carnage. The 1995 document reported that the feds had "forestalled a number of planned murders" by both sides.

The feds surveilled and searched family safe houses on both sides of the conflict, recovering more than one hundred guns. Bugs installed in cars and other locations provided the feds with a steady flow of details about the ongoing battle.

In one incident, agents rushed to Orena underboss Patty Amato's home on February 27, 1992, after learning of a Persico plot to murder their rival, only to discover that Amato was already in the wind. Amato finally surrendering after a month on the run to face his trial alongside Little Vic.

Court papers later reported that Amato's wife and their home were under federal surveillance for six weeks to thwart the Persico side's attempt to whack their target.

The war's luckiest combatant emerged as Orena soldier Bobo Malpeso, the survivor of three separate and unsuccessful April 1992 murder plots by Persico backer Michael Sessa and his crew.

The first attempt to kill Malpeso came when a hit squad spotted his white Lincoln Continental car parked outside a Brooklyn social club. The assassination was scrubbed when the plotters saw a suspicious-looking car on the street nearby. Believing the vehicle belonged to either the NYPD or the FBI, the gangsters drove to a nearby auto shop and dumped their weapons. Malpeso remained unaware of his brush with mortality. As it turned out, their fears were accurate: the feds had called in the cops to interrupt the plot.

The same crew returned to the same location several days later and spotted a car belonging to Bobo's girlfriend outside the same club. The would-be killers waited to see if Malpeso was using her vehicle, but their efforts were in vain: when the car pulled out, their target was not inside. And by the time they located Malpeso, he had already left the area.

Take three came one day later. The co-conspirators surveilled the girlfriend's home on multiple occasions until Sessa—using a set of binoculars—spotted Malpeso in his car. Sessa flashed his headlights as a heads-up, but their target was spared by making a sharp left turn and because of some miscommunication between the inept plotters.

A gunshot fired at the fleeing Bobo hit his back windshield, but he was uninjured, and Sessa was reportedly outraged by the failed attempt. Bullet fragments were found six months later by the FBI during a search of Malpeso's vehicle.

Bobo's luck didn't last: he was eventually convicted of four counts tied to the war and sentenced to ninety-five years in prison.

Authorities also implicated Sessa in yet another plot to murder Wild Bill Cutolo, this time with a crew of seventeen gangsters assembled for the proposed killing of Cutolo outside his girlfriend's Staten Island home.

The killing was thwarted by a hidden bug inside Persico associate Joseph Ambrosino's car, through which federal agents learned of the plot to kill the Orena captain, leading to Sessa's and a co-conspirator's arrests. The decision forced the FBI to shut down the recording device and give up the flow of information from the listening device.

Ambrosino was caught in another bugged conversation while bizarrely proposing the execution of two Orena soldiers with the use of a rented helicopter.

"Fucking shots coming out of the sky!" said enthusiastic mob colleague Michael DeMatteo of the plot, with Ambrosino—dubbed "Joey Brains" after once leading police to a mob social club—just as excited by the idea.

"By the time the call comes over, you'd be gone," he said with a chuckle. "You could see bullets! You get the guy on the highway, so no one would know where it came from."

The pie-in-the-sky plot never took place.

The not-so-sharp Ambrosino was involved in another strange incident before the shooting ever started. The gangster received a 1989 tip about detectives staking out his house, so Ambrosino asked his wife to move a load of weapons stored inside their home onto the back porch of a neighbor. The plan was to wake up around 5:00 a.m. the next day and bring everything back, but the couple overslept—and the neighbor had already found the guns and called the cops.

The mobster, like so many colleagues, eventually became an informant and took the witness stand against Vic Orena and Patty Amato. Among the tales Ambrosino shared once in federal custody was of a plot that involved a five-member hit team to target an Orena faction member. After waiting in vain, the frustrated crew drove to Coney Island and honed their marksmanship at the boardwalk "shooting gallery," then went for hotdogs at the original Nathan's Famous Hot Dog Emporium.

21

Waiting on the Edge of the World

With the war finally over, the mob family in complete disarray, and the trials already underway, one thing remained the same inside the remnants of the Colombos: the Persicos were still running things.

Reports had already surfaced about heir apparent Little Allie Boy's bright future in the fading family business, noting his coming release from prison. The Persico son's eventual promotion followed his acquittal five months earlier in a federal trial on charges from the war in which the late Greg Scarpa emerged as the key witness.

The Grim Reaper, only days before his death, agreed to meet with a Persico defense lawyer—and provided two affidavits clearing the defendant of any role in the Colombo conflict.

"In all of the meetings that I attended during the war with Persico faction members, Allie Persico's name was never mentioned by anyone," he declared. "There was no reason to mention Allie because he was totally uninvolved and unimportant. Allie has no power to give orders, permission, approval, or anything else."

The younger Persico returned to his dad's newly refurbished social club in Brooklyn's Park Slope, rechristened as the His and Hers Social and Athletic Club. And on January 8, 1995, the *Daily News* reported in a front-page story that Carmine's son had finally ascended to the seat once held by his father: "THE NEW BOSS" read the headline.

The designated replacement didn't enjoy much time at the top before his own legal woes emerged. The heir apparent eventually faced a life sentence as the city's Five Families continued their downward spiral and the feds continued their assault on the Mafia.

The news was no better in the Orena camp. With their patriarch behind bars, the two eldest Orena sons, Vic Jr. and John, came to the attention of government prosecutors. Already facing charges linked to their roles in the Colombo War, they were indicted for a new pair of alleged crimes. Vic Jr. was accused in May 1993 of running a multimillion-dollar gas bootlegging scheme on Long Island. He was also accused with sibling John in a separate indictment of operating a $600,000 loan-sharking operation.

"So now we're going to jail; we're looking at our families and saying we're never going to see them again," recalled John. "We had seven indictments—I had three, and my brother Vic had four plus a murder indictment."

The brothers were offered a deal: fifteen years apiece for their guilty pleas. They decided to fight, although John now acknowledges that they would have likely signed off on the agreement if the feds had promised a sentencing range of five to seven years.

The siblings, behind bars in Brooklyn's Metropolitan Detention Center, were joined by family capo Cutolo, the man who fired the first shots at Scarpa to kick the war into overdrive and was now locked up and facing his own war trial.

John Orena recalled a jailhouse get-together between the three, with the brothers declaring they were leaving the Life and the Colombo family—win or lose at trial. They were done with the mob, the backstabbing, the treachery of old friends and colleagues.

"We're not running away," he recalled telling a stunned Cutolo. "We're walking."

Their decision was questioned by dad Little Vic, who worried about his oldest sons' life expectancy after turning their backs on the mob.

"My father said, 'They're going to kill you,'" recalled Andrew Orena. "And my brother Johnny said, and my brother Vic felt the same way, 'I'd rather get killed on the street than get killed in a basement by one of my closest friends.' My mother had a big part in that—her faith, how miraculous."

Orena's sons, recalled brother Andrew, had seen the future of the Colombo family and realized they needed to cut ties with their past and move forward.

"Why were they done?" he asked rhetorically. "The reality of the Life was bullshit. It wasn't this honorable thing that my father sold them. All their friends turned rats. And the treachery involved as well. The minute my father got convicted, everybody scurried around and vied for the position, you know?"

The gas case followed a two-year federal sting operation, with Vic Jr. accused of conspiracy and tax evasion in a lucrative scam in which his crew teamed with immigrant gangsters from Israel or the former Soviet Union to collect a "mob tax" of up to 3 percent per gallon in return for providing "protection" to local gas stations.

The details of the probe were astounding. The FBI and the Internal Revenue Service established a trio of sham gasoline companies in Baldwin, Long Island, and the office adjacent to theirs was set up as a video production company that really served as a hub for the probe while authorities recorded all the illegal activity for posterity.

The feds undercut the mob's demanded cost for gas, setting off a price war and eventually grabbing 25 percent of the local market—ten million gallons a month, officials said. The sting was shut down after threats were made against the lives of the FBI undercovers, followed by the delivery of a large funeral wreath to their office with the message "R.I.P."

The agents attended one final meeting with the mob representatives in which the undercovers were ordered to enlist in the Colombo scam or die. The agents quickly signed on to ending the sting before the arrests of eighteen defendants in the scam.

Vic Jr. and his brother, while free on $1 million bail apiece, were looking at some very hard time.

"This is a significant crime scheme which shows some newer immigrants linking up with traditional organized crime to cheat both the government and the average citizen," said US Attorney Mary Jo White in announcing the arrests.

She added that some of the defendants had already fled the jurisdiction. The sons of Vic Orena had not fled.

The first bit of good news for the Orenas arrived in early 1994, although they remained unaware of the development. Agent Chris Favo approached his FBI supervisor to report several of the Persico-side combatants, after flipping to the feds, shared their beliefs that Scarpa was the beneficiary of a law enforcement source sharing confidential details about the ongoing war.

Scarpa crew loyalist Mazza had also flipped to become a federal cooperator in March 1994, filling in the blanks for prosecutors about the almost unbelievable deal between the agent and the mob killer. A second and similar tale from a codefendant of Greg Scarpa Jr.'s, in a separate drug case, alleged that Scarpa Sr. had provided defendants with paperwork warning of their impending arrests.

According to Mazza, Scarpa had bragged to him at one point during their time in the war of receiving information about the hideouts of Orena backers from a law enforcement source. Scarpa also took a call from his "'girlfriend,' as he called DeVecchio," with a warning of a plot by Little Vic's loyalists to execute him, adding that "they were very close" to making a move.

That same month an internal FBI probe of the veteran agent was launched, a game-changing development for the Orena faction in their looming trials, with defense attorneys now on the offensive and armed with this new version of the infighting.

The first beneficiaries were Wild Bill Cutolo and six associates in a Brooklyn federal courthouse prosecution nine months later.

Only days before Christmas 1994, the jury acquitted all the defendants of charges from the war after a two-month trial. The defendants' families and friends cheered as the verdicts were read. The defense attorneys had put DeVecchio and Scarpa on trial in a winning case that raised hopes for Little Vic's two sons and their quintet of codefendants in their upcoming prosecution.

"Thank you, Jesus!" shouted Cutolo's wife, her hands clasped in prayer, as the verdict was read aloud. "Oh, St. Jude!"

Cutolo had faced charges of murdering Colombo acting boss James Angelina in 1988, and all the defendants were cleared of scheming to kill their Persico rivals during the mob war.

"Merry Christmas to the world," the euphoric Wild Bill said outside court. "I've got the best lawyer. This is the best Christmas present ever."

The lawyers for Cutolo and his codefendants invoked the long-standing ties between the agent and his insider, arguing that the defendants were forced to protect themselves against the murderous Grim Reaper and his law enforcement partner during the Colombo conflict.

Defense attorneys resurrected the late Scarpa, arguing that his relationship with the FBI agent had basically helped foment the war, flipping the script in a case and providing cause for optimism as the Orena side anxiously awaited their own day in court only months down the road.

"I think the greatest reason for this verdict was the jury's realization that the government was permitting Gregory Scarpa to be the main agitator in this war, while keeping him as their informant," said defense attorney James LaRossa after Cutolo's acquittal.

Key testimony came from Salvatore "Big Sal" Miciotta, an Orena faction fighter turned government witness, although the details he shared under cross-examination only boosted the defense's case: DeVecchio and other FBI agents gave him approval to continue running his extortion and loan-sharking rackets while working as an informant.

The 350-pound ex-Orena faction member also acknowledged providing his brother with a $10,000 loan to buy 150 pounds of marijuana during that same time—and brutally assaulting a young aspiring priest in 1993, later claiming that the victim had disrespected his daughter.

The witness was soon booted from future services for the feds after collecting nearly $100,000 for his efforts. In 1995, Big Sal was charged with weapons possession while in the arms of the Witness Protection Program, and his scheduled appearance for the government against the Orena brothers and their codefendants was scrapped only weeks before the trial.

The Orena attorneys would become the beneficiaries of this new version of the war just five months later, embracing the DeVecchio defense and insisting self-defense was the only feasible option for their clients once the shooting started.

22

Waiting on a Sunny Day

While there was reason for optimism when the trial began in early May 1995, the Orenas' nerves were quickly jangled during jury selection. Defense attorney LaRossa, after winning acquittals in the previous Colombo trial, was again on the defense team when a stoic city bus driver with a law-and-order mien was seated on the panel.

The look on his face said conviction, and John Orena recalls the mood in the Orena camp was anything but upbeat.

"It didn't look very promising for us, I can tell you that," he said, reciting the other pending charges against him and younger brother Vic. "My brother and I, we're thinking, 'Are we fucked?' But look, we always had our hearts and we had that faith."

With the trial looming, defense lawyers requested a hearing to determine whether additional FBI reports on DeVecchio's association with Scarpa should be made public, alleging that earlier documents showed that the feds "turned a blind eye to Scarpa's activities . . . to create and further a divisive conflict which would enable the FBI to make, it hoped, dozens of arrests."

Federal prosecutors quickly dismissed the charge, responding in a legal brief that the expansive defense request was done to force the FBI into "abandon[ing] the informant program entirely, which defendants no doubt would relish."

Shortly before trial, in an unexpected twist, the feds revealed that their witnesses would include Christopher Liberatore and his father, Anthony, the one-time Orena faction backers responsible for the botched bagel shop murder. The pair, following in the now-familiar footsteps of their mob brethren, took guilty pleas in the days before the scheduled trial date in a deal where both agreed to testify against their former Colombo colleagues.

But the defense team's strategy received two boosts before opening arguments: the first with a switch in the trial's presiding federal judge. The original judge, Eugene Nickerson, was replaced by Edward Korman, who later observed at the trial that DeVecchio "had certainly crossed the line by a fairly long mark."

"I remember the marshal coming out, it was a woman marshal, and she says, 'You have no idea how lucky you are,'" recalled John Orena. "Korman was a great judge."

And then came the even bigger twist: one day before opening arguments, federal prosecutor Ellen Corcella sent a letter to the seven defense lawyers confirming allegations that information flowed freely between DeVecchio and the homicidal Scarpa as the war raged between the Orenas and the Persicos.

Rather than challenge the defense claim of a working relationship between the pair, she instead acknowledged the ties between the federal agent and his informant before the defense could even address the jurors less than a year after Scarpa's death.

According to the missive, DeVecchio actually tipped off Scarpa to a pending 1987 arrest of his son, Greg Jr., on a drug-trafficking charge, allowing the younger Scarpa to dodge authorities for nine months. The mobster was also provided with information about an Orena hit squad hunting for Persico backers, In June 1992, Scarpa loyalists Mazza and James DelMastro were warned about impending arrests and told to steer clear of their usual haunts.

There was more: the agent shared a tip that Little Vic was staying at his girlfriend's house in January 1992, shortly before Orena's arrest. An unsuccessful hit was planned but never pulled off. DeVecchio, the document said, also shared telephone numbers with Scarpa for two of his loan-sharking customers.

As a bonus, in the late 1980s DeVecchio alerted the Grim Reaper that his social club was bugged by authorities and in February 1992 told him that Persico backer Carmine Imbriale was cooperating with law enforcement.

The *Daily News* also reported that shortly after the war's December 1991 start, Scarpa advised the FBI agent that the conflict could end quickly if Orena was arrested or killed.

In fact, prosecutors allowed, the FBI man shared details with the mob killer on at least eight occasions during the battle for control of the Colombos.

The public airing of the unprecedented ties between the mob murderer and his FBI handler, like manna from heaven, meant the defense could—and would—argue that the feds actually allowed Scarpa and DeVecchio to instigate the deadly conflict between the warring factions.

More than a dozen other attorneys with clients convicted or facing future prosecution for their part in the mob conflict were suddenly gifted with a new defense as well, one that might win retrials or a walk for the combatants.

Corcella, in her preemptive strike during opening arguments, quickly acknowledged the ties between Scarpa and DeVecchio, revealing that fellow FBI agents had "blown the whistle" on the G-Man one year earlier.

"Don't be distracted or detoured by Scarpa," she urged the jurors hearing the case. "You are not here to determine if Agent DeVecchio was incompetent or guilty of a venality or if Scarpa compromised DeVecchio."

The FBI agent, she added, would "get his day in court . . . He was acting, however misguided he may have been, in what he thought was a law enforcement purpose."

Defense attorneys, their booming voices filling the courtroom, unloaded on the government and its "rogue agent." The men on trial were portrayed as the real victims, forced to respond in self-defense against the Persico loyalists in a Mafia battle sanctioned by the nation's preeminent law enforcement agency.

"This is one of the darkest days in the history of law enforcement in this country," said lawyer Gerald Shargel in his opening statement. "The idea that this was a war with two sides is nonsense. This war was sparked and fueled, believe it or not, by a special agent of the FBI."

LaRossa described Scarpa as a "crazed killer" before running through the exculpatory evidence revealed by prosecutors. The defendants, he asserted, "did nothing more than try to protect themselves."

Alan Futerfus, attorney for John Orena, echoed the allegations that Scarpa repeatedly benefited from his friendship with the federal agent.

"He's committed oodles of crimes and miraculously, he's never been arrested," said Futerfus. "Was he told, 'We don't want you, we don't want to mess with the likes of you'? No. The silence, ladies and gentlemen, was deafening."

The FBI agent's attorney denounced the charges as unfounded once the allegations against DeVecchio were aired in the federal courtroom, dismissing the prosecution as "a disgrace."

But the drama only kicked into overdrive once the trial began, when the younger Liberatore was summoned as the first witness against the Orenas and recounted the grim details of the early-morning murder of the innocent bagel shop employee.

"I went in, I had on a black leather coat," Liberatore testified, recalling how he then asked the store worker where the owners were. "He looked at me and said, 'What are you looking for them for?'"

Those were the last words the victim ever uttered. Basically, Liberatore explained to the jurors, "there was a standing order that you should just go out and shoot anyone on the Persico side."

Liberatore recalled his mobbed-up dad taking him to Colombo social clubs at age five, where the veteran gangsters offered tips on mob etiquette. He eventually dropped out of high school to run errands for crime family members.

Liberatore's testimony also included an admission to once shooting a teen who stole his brother's bicycle and an explanation of why he decided to flip to the feds: an order from a Colombo higher-up to kill another gangster inside a house of worship after the bagel shop murder.

"He suggested that there's an area where no one could see and he suggested I stab and kill him—in church, on Sunday," he said in a calm voice. "That's when I decided to come clean and take whatever happens."

The tide took a major turn for the defendants with the testimony of Andrew's old FBI acquaintance, Favo, who was summoned as the last witness at the racketeering trial. Favo dropped a bombshell when recalling DeVecchio's bizarre behavior on the night of May 22, 1992, when Orena faction backer Lampasi was gunned down at the height of the family infighting.

"He slapped his hand on the desk and he said, 'We're gonna win this war,' and he seemed excited about it," said Favo. "He seemed like he didn't know we were the FBI."

Mob chronicler Capeci described the pained look on Favo's face from the witness stand as "similar to one most people have when talking about going to the dentist."

Favo, under questioning by defense lawyer Shargel, shared his concern that DeVecchio had crossed the line by miles in sharing his inside FBI info with Scarpa and recounted the temporary order for the senior investigator to cut his ties with the mobster.

"I believed Lindley DeVecchio was not careful or was being completely careless," he said. A pair of fellow federal prosecutors echoed his account in their own testimony.

When pressed about his failure to report his suspicions about DeVecchio for more than eighteen months, Favo said it was very difficult to point a finger at the "well-respected" fellow law enforcer, an agent for thirty years and an FBI supervisor for ten of his colleagues.

"If I said this to somebody, they would take it about as well as I would take it if somebody came up to me and said my wife was unfaithful," Favo testified. "They would not believe it; they would never believe it."

Favo, when recently contacted about the case, declined to comment on his unprecedented decision to implicate DeVecchio or to share any thoughts on the whole episode.

"It is nothing personal, but I have been contacted by other writers over the years who planned books on this subject," he wrote. "I have explained what happened, but in the end, they are not interested in what I explain because it is just not sensational enough or fit the narrative that brought them to the project."

DeVecchio, asked recently about Favo, offered a cryptic response: "I could have gotten myself fired for what I was considering doing."

Old Orena frenemy Carmine Sessa testified as well, recalling his suspicions about Scarpa's dual allegiance during his run inside the Colombos.

"I've been around the guy many years and I saw a lotta things," he said. "A lotta guys getting killed and arrested and him escaping all the time. Nothing happened to him . . . I thought there might be something funny there and that there may be some truth to this."

Shargel, in a blistering cross-examination of FBI special agent Howard Leadbetter, noted that Scarpa spoke with DeVecchio on the day of Grancio's gruesome slaying, and again one day later, with the mob killer advising the federal agent that "peace was now impossible" because of the execution, without mentioning that he had pulled the trigger.

Despite the revelation that an FBI agent allegedly rooted for a particular side in the mob war, the mood at the defense table remained uneasy. But John Orena said that the family remained hopeful throughout, giving credit to sibling Andrew for standing strong during the darkest moments.

"My brother was a big part of our case," he said. "Not only was he working on my father's case, he was working on ours. He had everything in his head."

Jury deliberations began, and the panel soon posed an assortment of questions that left defense attorney Shargel feeling queasy. Andrew was pacing in the courthouse hallway when the lawyer stopped to share his dour assessment of the jury deliberations.

As Andrew recalls it, Shargel's message was blunt: "I've got to tell you something. I don't like the questions they're asking. They're close to a verdict. I think it's gonna go bad."

Andrew felt the same chest-tightening panic that had pre-ceded his father's verdict three years earlier. He decided to leave the courthouse entirely this time.

"Fuck it—I'm taking a walk," he remembered. "I gotta go out and breathe. I've got my rosary beads from Medjugorje. I said, 'Ya know, I'm gonna do a rosary to clear my head.' I go out there, and I'm walking around that park on Cadman Plaza, and I'm saying my rosary.

"I'll never forget: It was a dusky day, overcast, and all of a sud-den this beam of the sun comes down on me. I feel the warmth on my chest, and it takes away my anxiety. I think maybe God's just giving me the strength to walk back inside. And then I hear Gerry Shargel yelling, 'Come on! Come here!'"

Deliverance, in the guise of twelve jurors, awaited inside after a seven-week trial and ten hours of deliberations.

The panel had sent out a note seeking DeVecchio's written notes of a meeting with Scarpa inside the gangster's home at the height of the warfare. It was an unprecedented request, as no one had mentioned the document during the trial. Indeed, neither Korman nor the defense team were even aware the paperwork existed.

But it did. And now the jury, after correctly surmising during their deliberations that the paperwork should be available under the FBI's own guidelines, wanted a look for themselves.

Red-faced prosecutors scrambled to find what became known as the "Kitchen 302," a report on the private forty-five-minute meeting between the mobster and the G-man. Its contents were devastating: Scarpa informed his handler that there was no Colombo war. In fact, a supposed mob hit on Scarpa three weeks earlier was merely a case of mistaken identity and not a restart of the hostilities.

For John Orena and his brother, the revelation provided a ray of hope, an unexpected but definitely welcomed bolt out of the blue.

"Well, look, we always had God in our hearts and we had that faith," he recalled. "The reality of it, what you're facing and everything else . . . But we could use the Scarpa material, which was big."

Prosecutors, as defense attorneys demanded a mistrial for their failure to reveal the document prior to the trial, agreed to surrender the paperwork.

Korman's subsequent ruling was even better for the Orena brothers' cause: He would let the jury see the document and render a verdict. But if they found the defendants guilty, he would vacate the convictions and approve their motion for a mistrial.

The jurors reassembled behind closed doors to finish their work.

Even the good news was too much for Andrew Orena to handle. His nerves were frayed despite the judge's stunning declaration and Shargel's new-found enthusiasm. Andrew maintained his refuge outside the courthouse, similar to his trip to the bathroom before the verdict in his dad's trial, as the jurors reassembled for their deliberations.

The antsy Orena initially sat on a bench holding his girlfriend's hand before walking nervously around Cadman Plaza. And then he spied a friendly face emerging from the courthouse.

"I saw my uncle Bobby Barrett—he's a New York City fireman, all over 9/11, a hero," he recalled. "He comes out first, followed by my brother Peter and then Chris Favo. And Bobby shouts, 'NOT GUILTY!'"

The jury had just acquitted all seven defendants.

"They all believed there was a cover-up, and many jurors wondered how come DeVecchio wasn't indicted," said a triumphant LaRossa.

When the jurors emerged, they were quick to condemn the role of the FBI agent and blamed him for kickstarting the war.

"You're always brought up to believe in your government and the American way," said panelist Nancy Wenz, a thirty-four-year-old Queens resident. "If you can't believe in the government, what can you believe in?"

A second jury member, declining to give his name, offered his take: "This really knocks the credibility of the FBI. If the FBI's like this, society is really in trouble. It showed Scarpa was basically running free."

The victory was short lived for defendants John and Vic Jr., who were still facing jail time on their other charges. But when they returned to the nearby Metropolitan Detention Center, their fellow inmates had already heard about the jury's chorus of "not guilty" verdicts and greeted the brothers as conquering heroes.

"The building was shaking," John recounted. "Guys were hanging on the railings. It was like they saw hope, that somebody was acquitted. That we won. The [federal] marshals were so happy for us."

It was the start of a new chapter for the Orenas, particularly for John and Vic Jr. The pair's multiple federal cases, with long prison terms on conviction, were resolved after the DeVecchio paperwork was revealed, and both wound up pleading to lesser charges. Vic Jr. dodged a conspiracy-to-murder charge that would have come with a life sentence.

"Me and my brother, I wound up getting five years and Vic wound up getting seven," said John, still sounding a bit astounded by the turn of events. "When I went to jail, I was very spiritual. I said my rosary every day. And I did a lot of time, for four, five years, I put a lot of time into prayers."

And he recalled a jailhouse meeting with attorney Bruce Cutler, best known as boss John Gotti's blustering mouthpiece, who arrived in disbelief about their good fortune once the dust of their pasts was blown away and the plea deals approved.

"He says, 'What happened to you guys, I will never see again in my life. You're both facing twenty years on the RICO charges, and between the both of you, you get a dozen years?' That was like a miracle in itself," recalled John. "Cutler told us, 'Think about this for a second! Seven counts, at twenty years on each count!' He says, 'Between the two of you, you got twelve years! You'll never see that again. A miracle! I want you to remember that, because that's unbelievable.'"

The feeling of triumph faded quickly, though, as John and Vic Jr. went away to do their time. The namesake Orena was released on March 31, 2000, and his younger brother walked out of prison on July 31, 1998, their backs already turned on the Colombo family.

For Andrew, the verdict—with its implications involving DeVecchio and Scarpa—was like someone had opened a door to go back in time and resurrect his father's chances at overturning his convictions.

"I polled all the jurors, and they all said, 'Your father has to have a new trial,'" he recalled. "We even had a party. We invited them all, and a few of 'em showed up."

In all, nineteen Orena faction loyalists were either acquitted or had their convictions tossed over the revelations as the Scarpa/DeVecchio alliance became a go-to defense tactic on the legal side of the war—though Little Vic, despite his son's efforts, was not among their fortunate ranks.

Judge Weinstein, in hearing the subsequent appeals of Orena, Amato, and Michael Sessa, found that the Scarpa/DeVecchio defense would not have spared the high-level combatants on either side of the war.

"The notion that DeVecchio or the FBI fomented the Colombo war in a deliberate attempt to assist the Persico faction, or even tainted the investigation, flies in the face of the facts," he ruled. "Had the jury been presented with such a claim, it would have been shown by overwhelming evidence to have been demonstrably false and an egregious distortion of the record.

"As noted, the FBI and those agents DeVecchio supervised, as well as others, went to great lengths to prevent violence against either side in the war."

In retrospect, the victory at trial came as a somewhat melancholy gift for the Orena faction.

"It was a blessing for my brothers and a curse for Billy Cutolo," said Andrew. "Because my brothers did what they needed to do. They walked away from the Life. And they walked away from a lot of people they once knew and cared for. But they did it. They manned up."

Years later, Cutolo's decision to return to the Life after his acquittal would cost him his own. And despite the revelations at the Orena brothers' trial, the news for three other Orena faction members was not as happy after their own 1995 prosecutions tied to the war.

Acting capo Joey Amato was convicted as an accessory to the 1991 murder of the bagel shop worker that occurred at the onset of the Colombo war, and the jury was deadlocked on charges that Bobo Malpeso had dispatched the mob father-and-son hit team to the business.

Both dad Anthony and son Christopher Liberatore returned for an encore on the witness stand, their latest courtroom turn after spurning their old cohorts. The son testified in detail about six separate attempts to murder Persico backers during the war.

Malpeso was convicted alongside family associate Robert Gallagher for the June 4, 1992, attempted murders of mob rival Thomas McLaughlin and a fifteen-year-old innocent bystander, who was shot in the head while sitting on a nearby park bench. Both defendants were also convicted of conspiracy to commit murder during the Colombo war.

The jury deadlocked on charges that Bobo had dispatched the Liberatores to the bagel shop, resulting in the war's most notorious murder. The convictions followed a pretrial ruling by the presiding judge barring the defense attorneys from arguing that the ties between DeVecchio and Scarpa and the agent's sharing of information with his informant played a role in the violence.

Among the defendants cleared alongside the Orena brothers in their 1995 acquittals was family capo "Paulie Guns" Bevacqua, who reached out to Andrew Orena years later to ask for a meeting. Little Vic's son considered him an elder statesman inside the family and agreed to a sit-down in Great Neck, Long Island.

"I went out first to see an old friend of mine, he's a builder," said Orena. "And he says, 'Hey, Andrew, take a look at this device I have. It's crazy. If someone's wearing a wire on you, it will beep or vibrate.' He said, 'maybe you'll need it.' I said, 'I don't but I'll take it, put it on vibrate, thank you.' Then I grab my coat and I go to meet Paulie.

"I walk in, sit down and he goes to the bathroom, and the thing starts buzzing as he walks past me. And it stops when he walks away. I'm like holy shit! Paulie came back and later said he'd take care of the check. And I pulled out the device and tossed it on the table."

In 2011, Bevacqua was outed as a federal informant after wearing a wire to record his conversations with fellow Colombo members, including a family consigliere who was heard demanding a $150,000 payout from the Gambino family to cover the medical bills of a mobster who had been stabbed by a man linked to John Gotti's old comrades.

23

Wrecking Ball

In the months before the Orena brothers beat the rap in their trial, another prominent figure in the war had landed in the crosshairs of federal investigators: agent Lin DeVecchio, one of their own. The hard-to-imagine details of DeVecchio's unprecedented arrangement with Scarpa first emerged in 1994, when the FBI launched a probe that stretched over more than two years before reaching its resolution in favor of the veteran investigator.

There was by then some collateral damage as the story of the war unspooled. Former NYPD Detective Joseph Simone—who lost his job, his pension, and his good reputation amid allegations of working as an informant peddling inside information to the Orena side—was acquitted by a Brooklyn federal jury that same year after less than two hours of deliberations. The veteran cop, who worked on the elite NYPD/FBI Organized Strike Force, was accused of taking a $1,500 bribe to feed a mob member with information on the war.

Simone later said DeVecchio's second-in-command, Chris Favo, had ordered him and a second officer to end a surveillance before the gruesome killing of "Nicky Black" Grancio at the hands of a Scarpa hit team.

"The real criminals were the FBI," Simone declared. "Maybe now, someone else will see that. Maybe now, the real truth will comes out. . . . I wasn't afforded the benefit that Lindley DeVecchio got. He got his pension and immunity on everything."

Twelve years later, he also thanked a woman named Angela Clemente, a self-employed private investigator who emerged to take a deep dive into the Scarpa/DeVecchio morass, describing her as a "guardian angel." She would become as a key player in the case, and her work led to more legal woes for the federal agent.

The DeVecchio federal investigation, conducted by the Department of Justice's Office of Professional Responsibility (OPR), ultimately opted to bring no charges against the agent over his ties to Scarpa. The announcement came in a two-sentence letter released September 4, 1996, with a finding that the prosecution of DeVecchio was "not warranted."

But some damning details had emerged. According to court documents, DeVecchio's fellow law enforcers had initially believed "he was not pursuing the investigation as diligently and meticulously as he should have. It was not until several Colombo Family defendants agreed to cooperate with the government that more specific allegations . . . came to light."

By then, attorneys for Vic Orena were already arguing that their client deserved a new trial amid the postwar revelations, and a subpoena was issued for the agent's appearance at a May 1996 federal court hearing before Judge Weinstein. The revelations at the trial where Vic Jr. and John were acquitted loomed large as defense lawyers sought to revisit the federal agent's alleged role in the conflict.

DeVecchio's much-anticipated testimony instead lasted just four minutes: the witness invoked his Fifth Amendment rights and declined to testify beyond acknowledging he was an FBI agent. His response to questioning was simple: "On the advice of counsel . . . I cannot answer your questions because of my Fifth Amendment privileges."

Weinstein quickly called the long-awaited grilling of DeVecchio to a halt.

"Nothing is going to be gained by your asking him a series of one hundred questions," the judge told defense lawyer Shargel, adding that he didn't want the hearing to become a circus before dismissing DeVecchio as a witness. "He faces serious, possibly criminal, and certainly civil charges, maybe administrative."

Outside the courthouse, the Orena attorney expressed his disbelief about what had just happened inside.

"I've been practicing for twenty-six years, and I have never heard, read, or seen anything like this ever happening with an FBI agent," declared Shargel. "What I think this shows is that when the FBI had a problem, they circled the wagons. I think this information should have been turned over to the defense, and that our [other] clients deserve new trials."

A day later, the head of the FBI's New York Organized Crime Section testified about his instructions to DeVecchio about cutting his ties to Scarpa after the informant was accused of committing crimes while in the embrace of the feds.

Federal agent Donald North recounted how another FBI agent approached him in March 1992 with concerns about Scarpa's ongoing criminal activity while working for the feds. That led to a sit-down with DeVecchio about the allegation.

"He was adamant," said North of DeVecchio. "He was convinced that Mr. Scarpa was not involved in any criminal activity."

One month later, North said, he learned that Scarpa was reopened as an informant without his approval, noting that his OK was not needed for DeVecchio to make the move. Nearly two years later, three FBI agents working under DeVecchio came to North to share their concerns that the FBI veteran was leaking inside intel to Scarpa, leading to the initial report to the OPR.

Weinstein soon signed off on the release of more than one hundred pages of FBI documents dating from 1961 to 1994, laying bare to the public the ties between the two men, as well as Scarpa's long-rumored work for the FBI in the Deep South three decades earlier.

"Do you really think the FBI brought Greg Scarpa from Brooklyn, New York, to Mississippi for his investigative skills?" asked defense attorney Shargel.

The documents also included a 1981 memo citing Scarpa's unusual request to work with just a single FBI handler, rather than with the usual two. Along with the disclosures, DeVecchio's twenty-eight-page statement to investigators in the case was made public. In it, the agent insisted he had never crossed the line during his regular meetings with Scarpa across their twelve-year relationship, beyond accepting some gifts from his late informant.

"I established an excellent rapport with Scarpa, but I always remembered that he was a 'wiseguy' and I was an FBI agent," wrote DeVecchio, who explained his approach to the handling of all informants—and Scarpa specifically.

"The special agent's relationship with a confidential source is a special one," he explained. "He is always aware of the potential danger to his source as well as to himself, and he is always concerned about maintaining the trust of his source. Any special agent who handles a confidential source did so (and still does so) in a highly sensitive and clandestine way.

"The FBI encourages these clandestine relationships because the information derived from these sources is the lifeblood of its investigatory activity."

During Scarpa's time as his informant, DeVecchio assembled a seven-hundred-page file detailing their relationship, court papers showed. And the federal agent, speaking directly to his relationship with Scarpa, asserted that every conversation between the two was simply standard operating procedure for any FBI agent.

"At no time did I ever instruct Scarpa to murder anyone; nor did I ever conspire with him to plan any murder," he said in the statement. "I have never knowingly provided Scarpa with information which could have led to, or assisted him, in the murder of any individual."

DeVecchio was summoned a year later for another hearing in Orena's legal battle for freedom, again inside a packed Brooklyn courtroom. He was granted immunity before blowing up when asked directly by Shargel if he was a source for Scarpa.

"That's nonsense," said the irate agent. "That's absolutely incorrect. I was not the law enforcement source."

His fellow FBI agents turned out in support of DeVecchio at the long-awaited hearing, where they were joined in the audience by Little Allie Boy Persico and a pair of federal judges.

DeVecchio also disputed the version of events alleged by Favo involving his relationship with the Grim Reaper. And he said his FBI higher-ups were aware of reports linking Scarpa to multiple murders during the war, but they never told him to cut ties with the lethal mobster.

Assistant US Attorney Valerie Caproni followed him to the witness stand, describing the alliance between DeVecchio and Scarpa as "an awful, horrible sideshow"—but insisting that their relationship was insufficient to win Orena's freedom.

"There is a strong circumstantial case that DeVecchio leaked information to Scarpa," she testified. "We don't contest that. But so what?"

Weinstein eventually refused to throw out Orena's and Patty Amato's convictions in a 101-page ruling against the pair.

The mob duo were "proven by strong evidence to be murderous criminals," he wrote. "That [DeVecchio] had largely inadvertently fallen under Scarpa's spell and furnished him with some warnings to protect Scarpa personally and as a source is likely.

"That DeVecchio conspired with Scarpa on the side of the Persico faction or that he stirred up the war is not."

The veteran federal agent's attorney declared that the decision in favor of DeVecchio was "a long overdue vindication," while DeVecchio recalled decades later that both the initial probe and the latest one ended without criminal charges.

"They looked under my fingernails," said DeVecchio, insisting that the outcome was the right one. "Bank records, they found nothing. Not a damned thing. I was under the looking glass. I was called before a tribunal of agents, they grilled me. I said it's all bullshit. I never violated my oath of office. No information was ever given."

But Caproni, in a hint of things to come, said investigators had not exonerated the agent with their OPR probe, but rather they "did not believe they have proof beyond a reasonable doubt."

The thirty-three-year FBI veteran retired in October 1996 and soon sold his longtime home in the New Jersey suburb of Dumont and relocated to a quiet three-bedroom residence in sunny Sarasota, Florida, settling amid the palm trees. The ex-fed joined a local motorcycle club and served as president on the homeowners board in his neighborhood.

When the Fourth of July rolled around, he gathered with the locals to watch the fireworks burst over Sarasota Bay.

A decade after DeVecchio's departure, as he enjoyed a life of leisure, investigators 1,200 miles north in Brooklyn were taking a deep dive into the G-Man's storied past and the role he played in his work with Scarpa in an investigation that would stretch across thirteen months.

Little Vic's son Andrew was by then already working on his jailed father's behalf, lobbying members of Congress and arranging for a 2005 meeting with Congressman William Delahunt of Massachusetts in his efforts to refocus attention on the Scarpa/DeVecchio ties, arguing that their duplicitous pairing had spawned the war—and that his father should be freed.

"It took me about six months to get the sit-down," said Andrew, recalling how a local DA arranged for the meeting. "I was all over the book *Black Mass*, with Whitey Bulger and a crooked FBI agent. They knew this was identical to that, but worse than the Winter Hill Gang. This was the Italian Mafia."

Angela Clemente, a single mother of three from New Jersey, and forensic analyst Stephen Dresch, a Yale-trained economics professor, joined Andrew in his search for answers. Clemente's interest in DeVecchio came after receiving a 1999 call about the murder of Orena loyalist Minerva. Her attention soon turned to the tale of the rogue agent and his star informant as she and her investigative partner launched a deep and lengthy dive into the case, amassing a pile of documents and details shared with investigators.

"I never dreamed it would take six years," she said afterward, unaware it would take another long wait before her request for the FBI's unredacted Scarpa file was finally approved. Professor Dresch recalled spending months tracking down imprisoned mobsters and mob informants, including Greg Scarpa Jr., and poring over FBI documents and transcripts before the meeting with Congressman Delahunt.

Andrew first spoke directly with Delahunt's close associate John Kivlin, a highly regarded former Massachusetts prosecutor, and laid out his case against DeVecchio.

"I called the office and told him this was very much like Bulger—but worse," Andrew recalled. "We communicated over several months, I shared my documentation about the case, handled it myself. And one day the phone rings, my wife answers, and it's Kivlin on the phone. He says, 'Are you ready to meet?' And I said, 'Absolutely, I've been waiting.'"

Orena, with his attorney Flora Edwards, was joined by Dresch and Clemente for the gathering at Delahunt's Cape Cod office.

"He reminded me of one of the Kennedys," recounted Orena. "He had that status, an important man and a gentleman."

Delahunt told his guests, after reviewing their detailed information about DeVecchio, Scarpa, and the war, that he believed there was a viable case to be made against the retired investigator—but not in a federal court.

"He looked at Kivlin and said, 'Who's the DA in Brooklyn? That's Joe Hynes, right?'" recalled Orena, with the Grancio murder specifically mentioned. "And he said, 'You let me know. If they drag their feet, get back to me and I'll keep bothering them.'

"Ultimately, the Brooklyn DA found a lot more stuff and indicted him [DeVecchio] on multiple charges."

Clemente even received a shout-out for her efforts from Brooklyn prosecutor Michael Vecchione at the news conference in 2006 where the DeVecchio charges were revealed.

"See that woman over there?" he asked the assembled media. "She opened Pandora's box."

Once the charges were filed, Clemente became a target: she was found three months later, beaten and unconscious in a

Brooklyn parking lot where she had driven after finding an anonymous note on her car about the Minerva hit. No one was ever arrested in the case.

According to the investigator, she was met in the lot by a man with a single question: "Are you going to keep investigating DeVecchio?" When she replied yes, the man punched, kicked, and choked her unconscious.

"God bless Angela," said Andrew Orena at the time. "She's protecting more than Vic Orena or my family. Which is more dangerous? A gangster or a government that does anything it wants?"

She continued working on the Scarpa/DeVecchio case for years, eventually collecting more than one thousand pages of previously classified documents related to the Grim Reaper. Clemente later uncovered another stunning alliance, this one between the feds and mob hitman Frankie "Blue Eyes" Sparaco—a Persico backer and stone killer who admitted to five murders in the war and was sentenced to twenty-five years in prison.

Andrew did his own relentless digging, eventually garnering a list of FBI Top Echelon Informants in New York going as far back as 1971, including some of the biggest names in the city's long and lucrative history as the epicenter of the American Mafia. Their identities were shocking: "Big Paul" Castellano, legendary mob boss Carlo Gambino's son-in-law and successor; Aniello Dellacroce, Gambino's future underboss and mentor to the young John Gotti; Vincent Aloi, a close friend of Vic Sr. and a Colombo family stalwart who rose to the position of Colombo underboss.

There was one name missing among the most infamous of the federal government's top Mafia cooperators: Scarpa, who was recruited in the 1960s and thirty years later headed the faction that tried to kill Vic Orena. And the identity of another reputed informant would remain a secret held by Andrew for years until he went public with a shocking allegation that set off one last firestorm between the Orenas and the Persicos.

There was also a lawsuit filed by the family of Nicky Grancio in 2006 alleging that DeVecchio had called off the law enforcement surveillance team that had been following Grancio before he was executed by Scarpa, giving the killers a free shot at their target.

Their case, read court documents, "is about the corrupt and unlawful relationship law enforcement and a ruthless killer and career criminal that went unchecked for years and led to the cold-blooded murder of a man."

The former agent, through his attorney, denied the allegation. But there were more charges coming against DeVecchio, and the law enforcer soon became a defendant in a headline-making trial with a stunning and dramatic grand finale inside a Brooklyn courtroom in a scenario more improbable than anything ever conjured inside the fertile minds of Hollywood script writers.

24

It's Hard to Be a Saint in the City

On March 23, 2006, a Kings County grand jury delivered an indictment against the retired and once highly regarded FBI agent Lindley DeVecchio on four counts of second-degree intentional murder. The crimes were committed between September 1984 and May 1992.

Three days later DeVecchio flew from his sunny retirement home in Florida to spend the night inside a nine-foot-by-twelve-foot room at the Brooklyn DA's offices, with one of his wrists handcuffed to a chair. He recalled thinking—quite presciently—that the key witness in the case was likely to be Linda Schiro, the "mob moll" and significant other to the late Greg Scarpa.

On March 30 the FBI veteran, once uncuffed and inside the courtroom, entered his pleas of not guilty to the multiple slayings.

According to Brooklyn DA Charles Hynes, the retired federal mob-buster had assisted Scarpa in the quartet of murders by feeding his alleged partner-in-crime with confidential information about the doomed victims.

"On February 1, 2005, the Kings County District Attorney's office received a letter suggesting that [DeVecchio] was involved in the murder of Nicholas Grancio on January 7, 1992, in Brooklyn, New York," declared court papers from Assistant District Attorney Ann Bordley. "The District Attorney's Office was not able to substantiate the allegation that the defendant was involved in the Grancio murder.

"However, during the course of the Office's investigation, the office uncovered evidence of the defendant's participation in the murders of four other individuals: Mary Bari, Joseph DeDomenico Jr., Patrick Porco, and Lorenzo Lampasi."

The details in the indictment were beyond shocking, alleging that the agent provided Scarpa with Lampasi's home address before his execution. Prior to the murder of seventeen-year-old Patrick Porco, DeVecchio spent five to ten minutes in a phone conversation with Scarpa. The Grim Reaper then told his girlfriend that the teenaged target, a close friend of his son Joey, was an informant and about to inform on Scarpa's son, Greg Jr., for a 1990 murder.

"I can't believe this fucking kid. Patrick is going to rat on Joey," Scarpa was quoted as saying in court papers. "We got to do something about this."

Mary Bari was murdered after DeVecchio allegedly informed Scarpa about his fears that the attractive thirty-one-year-old would reveal the location where Carmine Persico's fugitive brother Alphonse was hiding out. Bari was forced to lie on the floor of the Wimpy Boys social club and was shot three times in the head, prosecutors alleged.

Alphonse Persico, the family's original "Allie Boy," first met Bari in 1969, when she was a sixteen-year-old high school student and he was a married man. Their romance ended fifteen years later, after Persico jumped his $250,000 bail before his sentencing on an extortion charge.

Authorities further charged that DeVecchio had collected weekly payoffs from Scarpa totaling more than $66,000 in return for his assistance to the murderous mafioso. According to court documents, DeVecchio would regularly collect a roll of cash tucked inside a rubber band as the pair conspired between 1987 and 1992.

It was, if proven true, perhaps the greatest betrayal in the FBI's storied history—and beyond.

"The most stunning example of official corruption that I have ever seen," said Hynes. "Four people were murdered with the help of a federal law enforcement agent who was charged with keeping them safe."

Hynes said his investigation revealed "a troubling path of confidential leaks, payoffs, and death."

The news was greeted as cause for optimism among the Orenas, who were still hopeful of their patriarch's unlikely freedom.

"I'm very excited about this," said Edwards, the lawyer for Little Vic. "And an [indictment] by the grand jury would certainly bear on the [earlier] convictions."

But Andrew Orena, despite his long wait for justice, took little pleasure in the agent's legal woes or the court hearing where DeVecchio was released on $1 million bail and was left facing a sentence that, if he was convicted, would ensure his death behind bars.

"Mike Vecchione called me to ask if I was coming to his arraignment," said Orena. "I didn't feel happy about him being indicted. It's clear the guy was involved, but he was accused of being a rat by another rat."

The DA received a bit of fan mail after the charges were unsealed—a letter from actor James Caan. The Oscar-winning

star, perhaps best known for his role as hot-headed Sonny Corleone in *The Godfather*, was close with Colombo family member
Joseph Russo, who was convicted in 1992 of murder and racketeering in a case involving DeVecchio.

"Joseph Russo is a dear friend of mine and I cannot express
enough how pleased I am that your office has taken an interest
and is in pursuit of correcting this problem," wrote the Bronx-
born actor. "Thank [you] for undertaking such an extensive and
malignant corruption case."

Attorney David Schoen, representing the Porco family in a
pending civil lawsuit against DeVecchio, expressed his shock that
a federal agent was now facing charges in connection with his
murder.

"Losing Patrick as a teenager ruined the lives of his entire
family," said Schoen, who would reemerge as an advocate for the
freedom of Vic Orena. "The family is stunned now to learn that
an FBI agent is allegedly involved in Patrick's murder. Stunned,
and they're looking forward to getting to the bottom of what
happened."

The alleged rogue agent was not without his supporters: former FBI assistant director James Kallstrom and legendary FBI
undercover agent Joe Pistone, of *Donnie Brasco* fame, came to
DeVecchio's defense as other colleagues launched a fund-raising
website to assist their colleague. At his first court appearance,
following his surrender and overnight jailing, DeVecchio saw a
phalanx of fellow feds who had turned out in a show of support
for their colleague.

DeVecchio uttered not a word as he entered the Brooklyn
courtroom and sat quietly as prosecutors charged him with four
counts of second-degree murder for acting in concert with Scarpa
in the killings.

Prosecutors alleged that the two men met throughout the Colombo war, with DeVecchio "counseling Scarpa to protect himself by eliminating imminent threats." And prosecutor Vecchione, head of the DA's investigations division, alleged that fellow FBI agents had already attempted to intimidate witnesses on behalf of the defendant.

Though the ex-fed was looking at twenty-five years to life if convicted, he sat impassively in a gray-checked button-down shirt, the top button undone, and a pair of dark slacks. The legendary agent, accused of sharing his confidential information for Scarpa's use in the war, posted bail and departed without a word after the extraordinary proceeding drew to a close.

"A complete fabrication," insisted his attorney, Douglas Grover.

There was more bad news for the retired G-Man: Scarpa's longtime girlfriend and confidante Linda Schiro had emerged as a key government witness in the killings of Bari, DeDomenico, teenager Porco, and Orena family loyalist Lampasi, and was set to share her account of damning conversations between the mobster and his FBI handler.

DeVecchio recalled his thoughts after learning Schiro would appear as a witness against him: "When Greg died, her source of money got cut off. There's no severance plans for mob spouses, and she got desperate for money. The Brooklyn DA was paying (a reported $2,200 a month for rent and food) for her testimony that Lin knew about this and that. Bullshit! But they took that at face value."

Among those in the courtroom were Lampasi's two daughters, who had traveled north from Florida to lay their eyes on the federal agent implicated in the execution of their father.

"I don't care if my legs go weak," said Mary Anne Lampasi, adding that their late patriarch had put them both through college and graduate school. "I will face this. It is harder to live not facing it. You can't run away from it . . . We were shielded. My father wanted us to have a better life than he had."

Prosecutors charged that the forty-four-year-old DeDomenico, one of Scarpa's partners in crime, was targeted in part over his decision to become a born-again Christian, a move the Grim Reaper considered just a single step from becoming an informant. And Lampasi's demise allegedly came after DeVecchio fed Scarpa the home address for his prey.

The damning document went further: DeVecchio "was aware of Scarpa's criminal activities, but he did nothing to stop them. On the contrary, defendant helped Scarpa and his associates to commit crimes and to evade detection by law enforcement agents."

Porco, the best friend of Scarpa's son Joey, was murdered just after the mob war began in 1991, and after the Grim Reaper received a call from DeVecchio, court papers alleged. He left home to make another call, from a pay phone, and spoke with the federal agent for several minutes. Porco was allegedly going to identify Joey in the recent murder of a teen outside a Brooklyn church.

Porco was instead executed and dumped on the street, and Joey Scarpa drove the car containing the corpse to its final resting place. The paperwork said Scarpa, in a meeting with DeVecchio after the hit, shared that the son was very upset over the killing.

"[DeVecchio] told Scarpa that Joey would get over it when he realized that, as a result of the shooting, he had avoided jail," the court papers declared.

25

Counting on a Miracle

The ensuing DeVecchio trial became a headline-making production, with reporters, relatives of the victims, and onlookers packing the seats inside a Brooklyn courtroom before the defendant entered the courtroom for opening arguments on October 15, 2007.

The city's tabloids were already splashing blow-by-blow accounts across their front pages in large print, offering a deep dive into the mind-boggling details. If convicted on all counts, DeVecchio faced four life sentences—one for each of the homicides.

The trial was preceded four months earlier by the final episode of *The Sopranos*, featuring boss Tony's fictional FBI handler delivering DeVecchio's memorable line "we're gonna win this thing" in the middle of the HBO mob's ongoing war as art imitated the Life.

As the trial loomed, prosecutors offered more shocking details of the alleged ties between the mobster and his handler: DeVecchio, in addition to the cash, received stolen jewelry and was treated to "the services of a prostitute" inside a hotel room on two occasions.

Greg Scarpa Sr. allegedly paid for the romps, prosecutors said, with a bottle of champagne included free of charge. DeVecchio later acknowledged receiving only a hard-to-find Cabbage Patch Kids doll from the informant for his niece and a dish of lasagna from Schiro one Christmas.

"One thing with wiseguys, if they offer you wine or lasagna and you say no, it's an insult," the agent explained decades later about the gifts. "There's no quid pro quo with that. Did they think I'm bought that easy?"

DeVecchio's trial appearance drew forty-five current and four retired FBI agents, their suits dark and their hair gray as they filled the seats in a show of support for their ex-colleague. A legal defense fund was launched in support of DeVecchio, who arrived for the session sporting a court-ordered monitor on his ankle.

More than one thousand agents from across the United States contributed to help their retired colleague fight the allegations, a sign to the accused FBI veteran of some light at the end of the legal tunnel.

"It was substantial, especially from guys who knew me, knew my work ethic," said DeVecchio in a recent conversation. "You can't fool the agents; if there's bullshit they can smell it. The whole thing was a house of cards built on bullshit."

DeVecchio opted for a bench trial at the last minute, despite encouragement from Justice Gustin Reichbach for a trial by jury.

"It is my determination that I want to have this trial in front of an impartial, intelligent individual," the defendant said. It was an interesting move, as Reichbach was known as a liberal judge who had been investigated by the FBI while a student at Columbia University.

The Orena sons never attended a day of the high-profile prosecution, just as they had skipped DeVecchio's first court appearance.

"I didn't think I belonged there," said Andrew. "I didn't want to be spiteful or seem any way like that."

Word of the allegedly corrupt G-Man reached as far off as Iowa, home to Senator Charles Grassley. The elected official weighed in over a reported dispute between the FBI and Brooklyn prosecutors over the alleged slow-rolling by the feds regarding their voluminous file on Scarpa.

"I have also heard that the local prosecutors in New York may have some trouble getting the documents from the FBI that they need to try the case," he said. "It is important that the FBI not take sides as an institution, just to protect one of their own."

The wildly anticipated case kicked off inside a Brooklyn courtroom with a full house for the morning's opening arguments. The dapper DeVecchio arrived in a gray suit, gray-striped tie, and crew cut, taking his seat for the first time in his long and storied career as a trial defendant rather than as a federal agent.

Prosecutor Joseph Alexis delivered his opening statement with a blunt assessment of the relationship between Scarpa and the defendant, declaring that the mobster used DeVecchio's tips "to devastating effect." He mentioned the late gangster's girlfriend, Schiro, as the key government witness, poised to detail the lawman's repeated visits to her home for damning sit-downs with Scarpa.

"Linda Schiro was the love of Greg Scarpa's life," he told the jurors. "Linda Schiro knew all of Greg's secrets."

The Lampasi killing, said Alexis, "was butchery. It was a massacre. What's predictable: Scarpa killed Lampasi. What's disgracefully shocking: the defendant helped him do it."

Defense attorney Grover returned fire in his opening, charging that Schiro's true motivation to testify was an infusion of cash from a book deal.

"She has taken real facts and real crimes and placed Lindley DeVecchio in the middle," he argued. "She has framed him . . . This is her final shot at a book deal, her final shot to make money."

And he defended his client's close ties with the Grim Reaper.

"Gregory Scarpa, as ugly and miserable a human as he was, a made member of the Colombo crime family, was a top-echelon FBI source," he declared.

There was also a bombshell charge contained in court papers filed by the defendant's lawyers as the trial began: mobsters allegedly conspired to set DeVecchio up after the federal agent helped put them behind bars in a plot to lay the blame for the Colombo war directly on the FBI agent as its instigator.

"We are going to paint this guy as the dirtiest fucking cop in the world," said Colombo family capo Anthony "Chucky" Russo, according to an internal FBI memo. "We have the money and the people to do it."

A spokesman for Hynes said the allegation would have "no impact on the case."

DeVecchio's estranged ex-colleague Favo took the stand to recount his fellow agent's excitement at word of the Lampasi killing during the Orena-Persico hostilities. The two had shared an office in FBI headquarters, he testified, but the two viewed the ongoing battle between the warring mobsters in starkly different ways.

Favo again testified to the agent's by now familiar reaction to the news of the Lampasi hit, in which the elderly victim was executed in a hail of bullets. DeVecchio then slapped his hand down on the desk, "chuckling, not laughing out loud, but laughing a little," said Favo.

"My impression was that when Supervisor DeVecchio said 'we,' he meant the Persico faction," Favo wrote in an internal memo. "He seemed like he didn't know we were the FBI or that he was not on our side. A line—it was like a line had been blurred."

Favo testified about his response to the strange remark: "We're the FBI! We're not on either side." And Favo also recalled a February 27, 1992, conversation where DeVecchio spoke with Scarpa about the arrest of Carmine Imbriale, a mobster turned informant, on the "Hello" phone—a secret line inside the FBI offices used strictly by cooperators to contact their handlers.

"The Brooklyn DA's got him," he quoted DeVecchio as saying. "I don't know what he's saying about you."

One day later, Favo recounted, he confronted DeVecchio about sharing information with Scarpa. Favo initially suggested that DeVecchio simply warn Scarpa that he had been overheard on a wire, and he eventually stopped sharing details of the case with his fellow agent before going to their FBI superiors with his concerns.

A second FBI colleague, supervisory agent Jeffrey Tomlinson, had already taken the stand to recall their suspicions about a rooting interest in the war. He testified how DeVecchio's fellow agents had withheld information of Scarpa's impending August 1992 arrest from their FBI colleague until the Grim Reaper was in already.

Tomlinson testified that Persico loyalist Carmine Sessa, after flipping to the feds, alleged that DeVecchio served as a conduit to Scarpa for details on the war. And Tomlinson confirmed that his concerns increased after overhearing snippets of a conversation between the agent and an informant on the secure FBI phone line.

The next witness represented the other side of the law enforcement coin: Larry Mazza, a prime member of Scarpa's wartime squad and a close pal of both the Grim Reaper and his girlfriend. The turncoat gangster, who shared a torrid romance with Schiro, estimated that Scarpa was involved in hundreds of killings, including more than fifty that he handled personally.

"He told me he'd stopped counting," said Mazza, describing his mob cohort as "a vicious, violent animal. He was just a horrible human being."

And yet, Mazza admitted, he once looked up to the late Scarpa and eagerly sided with his Mafia mentor and the Persicos in the war, giving up his aspirations to work as a cop or a firefighter. The two men met after Mazza slept with Linda Schiro. Mazza had been working as a grocery deliveryman, and Schiro later introduced him to Scarpa.

The young mobster and his lethal mentor were side by side inside a car when Orena loyalist Grancio was shot-gunned inside his car at the height of the war.

"By 1993, I was his confidant, his right-hand man, trusted," Mazza testified after turning government witness in 1994 and then spending a decade in prison. "You start out doing small parts of crimes. And little by little, you're asked to do more and more.

"Eventually, you're asked to be at the scene of a crime, then even commit a murder."

The tough guy killer broke down in tears during his testimony when he recounted his decision to give up his dream of following his father into the FDNY. He was followed by FBI agent William Bolinder, who dropped a bombshell on the witness stand: the mob had once pondered a plot to whack Mafia-busting federal prosecutor Rudolph Giuliani.

According to Bolinder, a 1987 debriefing report from DeVecchio recounted how Scarpa had shared details of the proposed hit suggested by Gambino boss John Gotti and backed by Carmine Persico. The heads of the other three New York families opposed the plot, apparently killing the scheme instead of the crime-buster behind the successful Commission trial prosecution.

The former two-term mayor, by then a Republican presidential candidate, joked about the report of a proposed hit tied to his reign as a mob-busting federal prosecutor.

"That was one vote I won, I guess," joked Giuliani in a subsequent radio interview. A jailhouse snitch had previously made the same claim, adding that back in 1986, Carmine Persico had proposed murdering two FBI agents—and Giuliani.

Bolinder's testimony continued, with the agent recalling how Scarpa had reported to DeVecchio that the Colombo hierarchy suspected that the Casa Storta restaurant in Brooklyn was bugged because FBI agents never surveilled any meetings of the mob held in the eatery.

The restaurant was, in fact, bugged, government records showed. Scarpa was ahead of the feds once again.

The stream of flip-flopping federal witnesses continued with Carmine Sessa, one of the quartet dispatched to execute Little Vic in the failed plot sixteen years earlier. It was a rare miss for the killer/informant, who found religion after thirteen admitted murders and a deal to turn on his old colleagues.

"I hate everything about the life I led, and I hope that it ends soon because it keeps destroying families and kids who are infatuated with it and can't wait to be goodfellas," he had declared at his sentencing in 2000, after joining Team USA. "I wish I could tell them what it really is."

Sessa did just that, testifying to Scarpa's disdain for the mob's oath of omertá, revealing that the Mafia veteran routinely discussed details of organized crime in front of his girlfriend, Schiro, and her daughter.

"I didn't know anyone to operate so openly," he testified, recalling that Scarpa spoke freely about all aspects of organized crime—even murder. And while there were suspicions about his duplicitous life, Sessa said he was convinced Scarpa was the ultimate gangster.

"He did so much work, how could he cooperate?" asked Sessa, explaining "work" was a synonym for murder. He described the late Grim Reaper as a liar and a notorious cheapskate, a malicious presence inside the Colombos.

The Orenas would later recall once asking Sessa why Scarpa wasn't killed by the Persico side and were told that his son, Greg Jr., had promised to flip to the feds, "and many of us would be dead" if they shared any details from their shared and lethal past.

26

Held Up Without a Gun

Linda Schiro, the government's star witness, took her seat inside the courtroom on October 29, poised to deliver the damning goods for prosecutors in their case against DeVecchio. She arrived for the day in a green knit blouse, a dark pantsuit, and a locket containing the ashes of her murdered son, Joey Scarpa, and took her oath to tell the truth before a packed house.

She recounted her first meeting with Greg Scarpa when she was seventeen years old and the pair crossed paths inside the Flamingo Lounge in Brooklyn.

"He told me how beautiful I was," she told the jurors. "He wanted my number, and I said no, I would call him."

Her new beau was soon boasting of his twenty gangland executions, she testified, recalling her odd reaction: "I wasn't upset. I was impressed."

Schiro recounted the tale of Scarpa's work for the government dating to the 1960s, including her account of accompanying him on a trip to Mississippi after the disappearance of the three civil rights advocates.

And she recalled specifically the interactions between Scarpa and DeVecchio, including how the agent counseled the mobster on people who needed to be executed: Mary Bari and others. Schiro recalled the gangster's gifts to the federal investigator—cash, a bottle of wine, and stolen jewelry—and the two men repeatedly sitting down inside the breakfast nook of the Brooklyn home she shared with Scarpa.

"If I had a problem, I could always call Lin because he was my friend," she declared.

But the bulk of her testimony across two days focused on the murders. Schiro matter-of-factly claimed she heard DeVecchio conspiring with the Grim Reaper to kill on four occasions and meeting up with Scarpa afterward to discuss the murders. In the Porco killing, she recalled, Scarpa learned from DeVecchio that his son, Joey, was about to be implicated by his best friend in the Halloween 1989 killing of a seventeen-year-old who was gunned down on the steps of a church.

"Listen to me!" she quoted Scarpa as screaming inside their home once off the phone. "Where this came from, it's high up."

According to Schiro, her boyfriend ordered Joey to murder his pal and that DeVecchio stopped by the house a short time later to learn that her son was an emotional wreck after pulling the trigger.

"Better he cries now than he goes to jail," she quoted the agent as saying.

DeVecchio sat impassively at the defense table during her testimony.

Schiro also testified that the mobster and the federal agent shared a laugh over how close to Scarpa's home Mary Bari's corpse was dumped after DeVecchio warned Scarpa that she was speaking with federal law enforcers.

"Lin just says, like, 'Why didn't you just bring the body right in front of the house . . . It was only two blocks away,'" she recounted. "Greg just starts laughing."

She appeared less confident while fielding questions from defense lawyers and the judge, mumbling at times and stumbling over dates. It was perhaps the first sign of good news for DeVecchio, with much more to follow when she returned to the witness stand a day later.

By the end of her two-day courtroom stint, the prosecution's case was in shambles. And DeVecchio would walk away a free man, turned loose in the most bizarre fashion imaginable and left to denounce the entire case against him as "a tainted witness, one witness, Linda Schiro."

27

Independence Day

Jerry Capeci and Tom Robbins were a pair of highly regarded New York journalistic veterans. Capeci was particularly known for his singular coverage of organized crime and his weekly "Gangland News" column, the city's home for inside news on the Five Families.

A decade before Linda took her oath inside the Brooklyn courtroom, the pair sat down for several long-forgotten interviews with Scarpa's significant other to discuss a book deal that never came to fruition. The tapes of their recorded chats remained stored away in a cardboard box tucked inside a closet—until they heard the details of her testimony against DeVecchio.

While Schiro's firsthand accounts of the four murders and the agent's role in them were both damning and devastating to the defense, her testimony was contradicted by the witness herself during her 1997 chats with the journalists.

The headline on Robbins's story that contradicted her new version of the multiple murders summed it up neatly: "Tall Tales of a Mafia Mistress."

"Linda Schiro, the key prosecution witness in the startling murder trial of former FBI agent R. Lindley DeVecchio, took the stand Monday, and it was hard not to find her story convincing," began the lengthy piece written by Robbins. "The first time I heard Linda Schiro, she also sounded convincing."

In the earlier interview, for example, Schiro told the journalists that DeVecchio played no role in the execution of Lampasi. But she testified that the federal agent had provided the murderous Scarpa with the target's home address as the three of them sat in her kitchen.

She even provided a motive, quoting Scarpa as denouncing "this fucking Larry Lampasi, he started rumors I am an informer, that I'm a rat."

The two reporters, as part of their agreement with Schiro, had promised they would not cooperate with any law enforcers seeking access to their conversations. But her first appearance on the witness stand convinced the pair to come forward with the recordings that had been a distant memory until Schiro swore to tell the truth in court.

"The story she told us then," wrote Robbins after her testimony, "is dramatically different from the one she has now sworn to as the truth. Lin DeVecchio may be guilty, or he may be innocent. But one thing is clear: what Linda Schiro is saying on the witness stand now is not how she told the story ten years ago concerning three of the four murder counts now at issue."

The first of their multiple interviews came on March 1, 1997, one day after DeVecchio was grilled by lawyers for Colombo family defendants attempting to get their cases overturned. And the resurrection of the details was enough to torpedo the DA's case—the DeVecchio prosecution was shockingly scuttled, imploded in an instant, when Schiro's long untold and contradictory tale was revealed in an unparalleled turn of events.

DeVecchio emerged as a free man, his reputation stained but the defendant unbowed.

"After almost two years, this nightmare is over," the ex-FBI agent said outside the courtroom after prosecutors abandoned their case in an appropriately stunning finish to the shocking criminal case. "It consumed me emotionally, drained me financially, and it has tested my faith in the system that I spent thirty years of my life defending.

"I will never forgive the Brooklyn DA. My question is, 'Where do I go to get my reputation back?'"

Schiro had appeared in the courtroom earlier, and Reichbach advised the star witness to hire an attorney of her own.

"If it's clear you gave false testimony under oath, you may be subject to criminal procedure," he promised, staring the witness the eye as she sat only a few feet away in the witness stand.

The former FBI agent and his wife, after celebrating at Sparks Steak House in Manhattan, headed back to retirement in Florida. The restaurant was an interesting choice—the site of the infamous mob hit on Gambino boss Castellano.

"We knew what her problems were, and it was important for us to corroborate everything she gave us," insisted prosecutor Vecchione after his case crashed and burned. "And we believed we had."

District Attorney Joe Hynes dismissed the disastrous prosecution as more of a "bump in the road" than a "black eye." Reichbach, before sending DeVecchio home, found time to denounce the former agent for "making a deal with the devil" in his alliance with Scarpa.

"There was no evidence presented at this trial save the discredited testimony of Linda Schiro that the defendant committed any of the acts as charged in the indictment," said Reichbach. "On the other hand, credible evidence was presented that indicated the defendant was so eager to maintain Scarpa as an informant that he was willing to bend the rules, including sending misinformation to headquarters to reopen him as an informant."

The verdict was crushing for the Porco family. Older brother Michael Porco had appeared each day of the DeVecchio trial to take his seat inside the Brooklyn courtroom. The case was a long time coming, and the sibling had waited seventeen years for someone to face charges in the killing.

"My parents would have wanted me to be there," he explained. "It's like dragging my body across New York City and all over the place all over again."

Schiro, in her brief appearance on the witness stand, had recalled Porco as almost like family, a familiar figure inside the home she shared with Scarpa. But the star witness had flamed out, and the prosecution was now a pile of rubble.

"The DA here did not take the simplest steps to verify what this mercenary and absolutely amoral human being was telling them," said DeVecchio lawyer Grover, dismissing the prosecution as "a model of what a responsible prosecutor should not do."

A civil case against DeVecchio accusing the federal agent of assisting in the Colombo war murder of Nicky Grancio after the victim's relatives had alleged that Scarpa had reached out to his handler to arrange the removal of an FBI surveillance team in the area prior to the murder was dismissed by a federal judge in July 2008.

"I've been vindicated in both venues, both civilly and criminally," said DeVecchio after the later ruling came down.

As it turned out, Schiro had also sat for an October 1994 chat with FBI agents in which she recounted meeting Scarpa as a teen and spending the next twenty-eight years living with the fearsome mobster. An FBI document detailing what happened provided a wildly different take on her boyfriend's relationship with DeVecchio.

"Schiro advises she never recalls Scarpa Sr. ever saying he learned any information from SSA DeVecchio regarding the individuals he was alleged to have killed or attempted to kill," the paperwork read. "Schiro advised Scarpa Sr. did not need any assistance in locating any of these individuals as he could easily find them.

"Schiro advised that Scarpa Sr. never told others in her presence that his law enforcement source/FBI source ever told him any specific information. . . . Schiro believed that the shooting of individuals during [the] course of the Colombo Family War was done on the 'spur of the moment' and did not take a great deal of planning."

In October 2008, a special prosecutor ruled that Schiro would not face perjury charges for her turn on the witness stand. And five years after the prosecution went down in flames, Brooklyn federal court Judge Edward Korman shared his thoughts about DeVecchio's escape from charges while sentencing Scarpa's son, Greg Jr.

"It was my view and remains my view that Lin DeVecchio provided information to Scarpa [Sr.] that got people killed," said Korman, who presided over the 1995 trial of the Orena brothers. "I found it pretty outrageous. And the bottom line was, of course, nothing happened to Lin DeVecchio. He was permitted to retire, and in his retirement was actually doing background checks for the [FBI]."

Scarpa Jr. was seeking a reduction in sentence in return for his efforts to help federal officials discover explosives hidden inside the home of Oklahoma City terrorist bomber Terry Nichols.

And federal judge Charles Sifton, later presiding over the cases of Orena defendants seeking new trials based on DeVecchio's role in the war, lobbed his own shot at the federal agent.

"Scarpa emerges as sinister and violent and at the same time manipulative and deceptive with everyone, including DeVecchio," he observed. "DeVecchio emerges as arrogant, stupid, or easily manipulated but, at the same time, caught up in the complex and difficult task of trying to make the best use of Scarpa's information to bring the war to an end."

In yet another of the bizarre incidents surrounding the war, Greg Scarpa Jr. appeared on a special video hookup from behind bars in January 2004 to implicate his father and DeVecchio in framing Orena for the murder of Tommy Ocera.

The namesake son, serving forty years for a racketeering conviction, spoke as Judge Weinstein presided over a hearing where he was flanked by seventeen boxes of old case files. Scarpa Jr. testified in an effort to win Orena's release, appearing at the behest of Little Vic's attorney Flora Edwards to revisit his father's work for the feds during the Colombo war.

"I am getting the truth out, just to get the truth out," he testified after submitting two affidavits on behalf of Orena. "The story that Ocera was killed on Orena's instructions was invented after the fact by my father and DeVecchio."

In fact, he testified that the federal agent collected a $100,000 payoff for his efforts on behalf of the Persico side.

Two weeks later, Weinstein again found there was no significant evidence to overturn Orena's convictions or those of his associate Patty Amato, despite the "seamy aspects of law enforcement" revealed in the years since the war. The younger Scarpa, Weinstein noted, had not personally witnessed the alleged corrupt ties between the agent and his father.

28

Living in the Future

More than three decades later, with the Five Families largely defanged in the new millennium, the hostilities between the Persicos and the Orenas endured, even as the sons of Carmine and Little Vic followed dramatically different paths in the postwar world.

Vic Jr., Johnny, and Andrew embraced a new life far removed from the world of organized crime, working in the legitimate world, living in the suburbs, and raising their families.

On the Persico side, Little Allie Boy faced a series of indictments after following his jailed father to the postwar Colombo seat of power in the years after the war. In January 2001, he was indicted again on the day he was scheduled to walk out of prison on a gun charge—this time for loan-sharking and extortion.

Persico took a plea deal in which he forfeited $1 million of his ill-gotten gains and was excoriated by the sentencing judge before heading back behind bars.

"There is no crime he wouldn't commit," said federal judge Reena Raggi after ordering the gangster to thirteen years at his November 2003 sentencing. "I'm not sure whether anything but incarceration for the rest of his life would deter Mr. Persico from continuing criminal activity."

Her words proved prescient: one year later, the jailed Persico was charged in the 1999 murder of Wild Bill, and a life sentence was imposed on the college-educated killer following his conviction in 2007. An earlier prosecution ended with a hung jury, whose jurists recounted Persico glaring at the panel and occasionally raising a finger to his head in an apparent shooting gesture.

"It's sad for the defendant and his family, but it was a choice he made," said federal judge Joanna Seybert, describing the Cutolo killing as a cold-blooded business decision and putting Little Allie Boy behind bars to die. "His intelligence and personality might have served him well in legitimate business."

Andrew Orena recounted his last meeting with Wild Bill, which took place inside a Brooklyn flower shop, where Cutolo explained how the fences were mended with the Persicos. But Little Vic's son was convinced that the old adage of the mob forgetting everything but the grudges applied to Cutolo.

"He says, 'Look, I went back in the family, it's going to be beautiful; there's not going to be any trouble here. Allie promised me Junior is our father,'" recalled Andrew. "Like he's our God or something. And I said, 'Billy, can I be honest with you? You're gonna get killed.' And he said, 'No, no, no, it's a new day and a new dawn. The violence is over with.'

"And I said, 'Billy, they're never going to forgive and they're never going to forget. Why don't you do what my brothers are doing? They're leaving the Life, they're moving on.' And that was the last conversation I had with Billy."

The next time Andrew heard about Cutolo was from a front-page story in the *New York Post* reporting his disappearance.

"It was like *The Godfather*, and I called my brother Vic and I said, 'Billy is missing,'" said Andrew. "And he said, 'Ah, he's gone.' It was so sad but poignant, because we had a soft spot for him."

Cutolo's long-buried remains were discovered in 2008, his corpse wrapped in a tarp with his Italian loafers still on his feet. Details later emerged that his hit was ordered at a meeting of mafiosi inside the rosary garden of a Long Island church. Seven years earlier, a surrogate court judge had declared Cutolo as legally dead.

Wild Bill's misguided belief in a détente with the Persico crew followed the 1994 acquittal in the first defense case to use the Scarpa/DeVecchio defense. Cutolo, with his new lease on life, sadly returned to his old life inside the Colombo family and the Persicos—but not for very long.

Five years after he walked free, Cutolo was bumped up to Colombo underboss as a gesture of peace inside the family following the release of Little Allie Boy from prison.

Things changed when Persico was convicted for gun possession in Florida, with the boss reportedly worried about Wild Bill moving to seize control of the family in his absence and ordering his death.

A prosecutor said the murder was also payback for Cutolo's active role inside the Orena faction during the war, describing the killing as "revenge served ice cold years later."

After the mobster's execution, his family was threatened and warned not to cooperate with authorities. They instead joined the federal Witness Protection Program two years later and helped convict the killers. It was, in an appropriate twist of fate, Cutolo's son, William Jr., who helped put the killers away, wearing a wire for seventeen months while gleaning information that landed more than a dozen mafiosi behind bars—including Little Allie Boy Persico.

"I loved him so much," William Jr. later said of his father. "During the war, I willingly would have risked my life for him. I'm his son. I didn't want to let him down again."

The mobster, known for his weekly haircut at a Bensonhurst barber shop and an annual appearance as Santa Claus at a local Christmas party, was last seen heading to a meeting with Allie Boy. The mob boss was convicted of Cutolo's execution, alongside codefendant John DeRoss, who was also found guilty for threatening Cutolo's wife and children.

The heyday of the Five Families were by then far in the rearview mirror, and the Colombos remained a shell of themselves in their glory days. Teddy Persico, a nephew of Carmine's, copped a 2023 plea for racketeering amid reports he was about to become the Colombo boss. His replacement emerged as Robert Donofrio, an Orena faction loyalist who switched allegiance to the Persico side in the war and wound up getting an eight-year sentence.

And Colombo veteran Vincent "Vinny Unions" Ricciardo was sentenced to fifty-one months behind bars in February 2024 for extorting cash payments from a union official. Authorities recounted his expletive-filled rant regarding the potential victim.

"I'll put him in the ground right in front of his wife and kids, right in front of his fucking house," he declared. "You laugh all you want, pal, I'm not afraid to go to jail. Let me tell you something, to prove a point. I would fucking shoot him right in front of his wife and kids."

The Orenas, in addition to their dad's woes, endured another family blow when Joan passed away in August 2013, with her husband still behind bars.

"She was a prayer warrior for her husband and her sons," said Andrew. "I feel it was my mother's prayers that saved my father's life and changed us all, you know?"

There was hint of the old days of the New York mob following the March 13, 2019, shooting of reputed Gambino family head Frank Cali. The boss was whacked in the driveway outside his red brick Staten Island home, making front-page headlines and sparking mass speculation about the start of a new mob war in the new millennium.

Cali, the fifty-three-year-old son of Sicilian parents, was born in New York City and was living in the same ritzy neighborhood where his murdered family predecessor "Big Paul" Castellano once resided in a multimillion-dollar mansion known as the "White House." Cali, after ascending to the boss's seat in 2015, came outside around 9:15 p.m. after a young stranger repeatedly slammed his truck into the victim's parked Escalade, knocking its rear license plate to the ground.

Video captured Cali approaching the man, who was sporting a baseball cap and hoodie. The killer handed Cali the loose plate, then riddled the boss with ten bullets to abruptly end a minute-long chat. Cali died at a nearby hospital, and the killer remained in the wind as headlines screamed of a possible organized crime hit.

The truth was more benign: accused killer Anthony Comello, twenty-four, was arrested three days later while on the run in Brick Township, New Jersey. His fingerprints were on the license plate, but his motivation was not linked to the Gambino family.

Comello explained that he was stoned after smoking marijuana nearby and actually apologized to Cali before the victim uttered his final words: "What are you, fucking kidding me? You don't know who I am. I could have you killed. You're lucky I don't kill you right here and now."

29

Land of Hopes and Dreams

The wages of the long-ago war came with different costs for different combatants, from the top of the Colombo family down to its street fighters. The disparity was best illustrated by the sentences handed down against the Sessa brothers for their roles with the Persico faction.

The saddest case belonged to Michael Sessa, imprisoned longer than even Little Vic, who was still filing court papers three decades after his conviction in a failed bid for his freedom.

One five-page court document filed on his behalf noted that his brother, Carmine, once Little Vic's turncoat consigliere, served less than five years after admitting to multiple murders, including the one that kept Michael behind bars. His friends and family were left to express their outrage over the disparity, with one friend submitting a November 2023 list of a dozen mobsters who received far less jail time despite their roles in the war.

"I am deeply concerned about the pattern of conduct that has been demonstrated toward Mr. Michael Sessa," wrote one supporter. "Sessa's older brother Carmine Sessa . . . admitted to being a leader in the Colombo family, admitted to committing 15 murders. . . . Every person that that comes before the court is to be treated with respect, to be treated fairly, to be treated with dignity and to be treated with compassion."

Sessa's sister-in-law, in a January 2024 letter, expressed her outrage at the latest rejection of his bid for compassionate release, citing 135 letters sent in support of his freedom, and noting that the jailed mobster's daughter was a five-month-old when he was arrested—and was now age thirty-two.

"When it came to Michael, you showed absolutely no compassion, no mercy, and actually were vindictive, knowing you were also crushing . . . my family's heart," she wrote. "Everyone is convinced that you have discriminated against Michael."

Sessa, acting as his own attorney, had argued in earlier court papers for a sentencing reduction or a new trial, citing the leniency shown to the stone-cold killer Scarpa and the crimes committed by his fellow Persico fighters in one appeal.

"The disparity in sentencing in this case is astronomical and a clear violation of the Equal Protection law," he wrote. "Joseph Ambrosino, a three-time felon and convicted of perjury, received five months in prison for the same crime as Sessa. And Carmine Sessa pleaded guilty to the same [murder] as [Michael] Sessa, plus 14 other murders, and was sentenced to 60 months.

"On the other hand [Michael] Sessa who never had a felony conviction before and self-surrendered was sentenced to life without parole. In fact, Sessa has already served more than 50 times [more than] Joseph Ambrosino and Carmine Sessa."

His sibling, Carmine, after flipping outside the midtown church, found redemption as a damning government witness against his former colleagues inside Scarpa's Wimpy Boys social club.

On September 28, 2000, seven years after his brother's sentencing, Carmine walked away a free man following a Brooklyn federal court hearing, his likely sentence life imprisonment reduced to time served. Sessa appeared as a federal witness in eight trials involving the Genovese and Colombo crime families.

"I hate everything about the life I led and I hope it ends soon, because it keeps families and kids who are infatuated with it and can't wait to be goodfellas," he later declared. "I wound up growing up around a life that was and is I wish I could tell them what it really is."

Few, if any, benefited more than the lethal Gravano after his admission to nineteen murders once in the embrace of prosecutors after becoming a federal witness. Sammy the Bull became a social media superstar, with a huge following on Facebook and Instagram and with multiple YouTube videos—and Gravano merchandise is available through his website.

The twenty-first-century mob was by then already well into its long war of attrition, its elderly ranks thinned by death and incarceration and the aging and imprisoned survivors arguing for their own compassionate release in lengthy court filings that focused on their failing health.

Front and center were the two leaders from the 1990s war, each waging a battle for a final taste of freedom before their almost inevitable deaths behind bars. The twin fights to win release for Vic Orena and Carmine Persico were conducted in court filings and legal arguments. The years passed as both families waited in vain for good news that never came.

Attorneys for Junior and Little Vic argued ardently for compassionate release, citing the myriad health problems of the old and ailing bosses. And neither received any compassion from the federal government.

The elderly Persico spent the last thirty-two of his eighty-five years behind bars and passing away at the Duke University

Medical Center in 2019, his efforts for a final taste of freedom falling on deaf ears long after the war he launched from behind bars was over and largely forgotten in the new millennium.

Junior, in a last-ditch bid for release before his death, had filed a lawsuit against the prison warden and a doctor alleging "deliberate indifference" to his medical issues, including a leg infection that left him at risk of amputation above the knee.

Three years earlier, Persico's attorneys had argued for his freedom by listing an assortment of medical woes and by accurately assessing his triple-digit prison term as a "virtual life sentence." A lengthy June 2018 court document filed on Persico's behalf argued that the aging mob legend, paying for the sins of Scarpa and DeVecchio, deserved a chance to go home.

"Unbeknownst to the sentencing judge, the allegations considered against Persico were based largely on a rogue FBI agent and his informant [Scarpa]," read the appeal. "Suffice it to say, had any of this information been revealed at sentencing as it should have, Mr. Persico would not have been sentenced to 100 years in prison. . . . There can be little doubt that Mr. Persico was treated in a way that that runs afoul of everything our criminal justice stands for.

"Surely justice will not be served by having Mr. Persico spending his final days imprisoned as a result of a sentence that was ramped up by false allegations."

During his stay behind bars, the old mob boss became friendly with a fellow notorious New Yorker: Ponzi scammer Bernie Madoff.

By most accounts, Persico remained a force inside the Colombo family, though his plans to keep son Little Allie Boy in the seat atop the mob were laid to waste by federal prosecutors.

Inmate Little Vic re-embraced his Catholic upbringing while behind bars, serving as a Eucharistic Minister giving Communion to his fellow inmates at a federal prison in Florida. The mob veteran, his hair turned silver, worked to recruit others to his jailhouse ministry, counseling fellow prisoners and inviting them to join a rosary group inside the high-security facility.

Andrew described his dad as a new man and insisted yet again that his father was wrongfully convicted on charges from the war. His codefendant and underboss Pasquale "Patty" Amato never made it home, dying at the age of eighty inside a Florida federal prison in March 2015.

In April 2016, Andrew sent a long letter to Judge Weinstein—now in his nineties and still presiding on the federal bench almost a quarter century after Vic Orena Sr. was convicted and sentenced inside his courtroom. He, too, was fighting for a second chance for his beloved pop.

"Your honor, I'm not a crusader against our government," he wrote. "I love my country and I also hate organized crime of any sort, it's an evil that destroys families and ruins young lives [who] want to emulate these fraudsters. I'm a son who loves his father and in all fairness realizes that had all this information been disclosed at his trial [it] would not only [have] led to his acquittal, but the case would have been thrown out.

"None of us can give back to the defendants the years they spent in prison," he concluded. "[But] we can be part of changing their future . . . and to see my Dad—who has lost everything worldly, including his wife, daughter-in-law, health and position—enjoy the time he has left surrounded by his sons and grandchildren who hardly know him."

The impassioned plea fell on deaf ears, but Andrew Orena refused to give up the fight. The brothers don't get to visit the patriarch much at the Federal Medical Center in Devens, Massachusetts, but they speak with him frequently.

"His heart is weak. But his spirit is strong. We're praying we can get some time with him. He has grandchildren that really don't know him," he told the *Daily News* in 2021. "He'll never be the man he was but he's still our father and we love him."

The Orenas had filed unsuccessfully for his compassionate release that same year, invoking the name of DeVecchio and insisting that his behind-the-scenes work for the Colombo family faction lured Orena into the bloody war. The government covered up the FBI agent's and Scarpa's roles, the family's attorney argued, alleging that the two conspired to instigate the war.

But while the government acknowledged Orena's poor health "arguably met the threshold of an extraordinary and compelling reason" for release, the appeal was eventually rejected.

The family's fight became a war of attrition, while Little Vic's condition continued to worsen. His medical woes eventually gave way to mental health issues, and a Brooklyn federal court hearing revealed that Orena was convinced he was the president of the United States.

"The delusions have been there for a while," said family attorney David Schoen. "Mr. Orena does not know where he is or who he is."

Yet the Orena sons never surrendered in their battle to win Little Vic's freedom over the decades. The imprisoned boss's family grew to include twenty grandchildren while their patriarch languished behind bars, his condition steadily deteriorating.

And then the Orena faction went back on the offensive in their long-running battle against the Persicos, leveling a bombshell charge that again set off fireworks between the clans.

In August 2021, thirty years after the war began and shortly after the anniversary of the long ago failed hit on Orena, with

Little Vic still behind bars and Persico now gone, Andrew Orena and attorney Schoen charged that the venerable Colombo boss, like Scarpa, had actually been working as a mob informant.

"SNAKE WAS A RAT!" screamed the page one headline in the *Daily News*. "Mob Boss Persico Spent Decades as Fed Source: Court Records."

Schoen filed the documents alleging that the revered Persico was also a "Top Echelon Informant" for the FBI, one of four Colombo family members mentioned in a November 1971 list of turncoats.

"I think it changes the entire dynamic of how this so-called Colombo war has been sold," said Schoen, after submitting his paperwork. "I never wanted to disclose this document. I think it potentially puts people in danger."

The list was uncovered by a Freedom of Information Act lawsuit filed by the attorney, who cited the paperwork as further evidence that the long-imprisoned Orena deserved to spend his last days with family.

The Orena attorney said he heard from a Colombo associate asserting his claim was "100 percent right." Schoen insisted that the man, a mobster turned cooperator, spilled the beans after testifying against a pair of Schoen's clients.

Schoen further stated that he had met with Inspector General Michael Horowitz of the Department of Justice, two FBI agents, and other officials to confirm that his interpretation of the document was accurate. Back in January 2015, John and Andrew Orena had sat down with Horowitz inside the DOJ building in Washington, accompanied by Schoen, who was then representing Michael Sessa.

Security was tight and the meeting was conducted under complete secrecy. Andrew carried a collection of documents compiled through years of digging, including the 1971 Top Echelon Informant list.

"They did not indicate they had any reason to believe it was anything than what it was purported to be or that any information reflected on it is inaccurate," said Schoen. "This explains a great many events, both directly related to Mr. Orena's case and otherwise."

The Orena side once more challenged the long-held narrative of the war, insisting that the last of the lethal Colombo conflicts was actually fomented by their one-time partners in organized crime and the FBI agent.

"The 'official boss' of the Colombo family, on whose side Scarpa and DeVecchio were working, Carmine Persico, was himself, since decades earlier, in the government's employ as a member of its 'Top Echelon Informant Program,'" wrote Schoen. "This explains a great many events, both directly related to Mr. Orena's case and otherwise."

Schoen said that Persico's cooperation made the Colombo "war" more of a one-sided "attack."

"It seems like perhaps it was being orchestrated from the top," said Schoen, arguing in the stunning court papers that Persico's cooperation was another factor in favor of turning the octogenarian Little Vic loose to enjoy a last taste of freedom.

Outraged attorneys who once represented the late Persico unleashed their instant ire at the shocking allegation.

"This story is BULLSHIT!" read an angry tweet from defense lawyer Matthew Mari, who woke a vacationing reporter at 7:00 a.m. to vent his outrage when the story ran. "Calling Carmine Persico a rat is like calling George Washington a British spy! Junior was a great client, man, and friend. The government railroaded him and he fought back like a MAN!"

Fellow Persico attorney Anthony DiPietro, who had battled in vain to win his client's possible compassionate release prior to his death, was equally incensed over the report.

"There is no truth to this allegation and the supporting record is substantively worthless," he said. "Having served as Carmine's lawyer, I can attest that he was not an informant, nor did he provide information to the Government.

"Until this day, Carmine remains a giant among men, and I was honored to represent him in the many contentious legal battles he fought against the Government."

Years later, Andrew Orena recounted the shitstorm following their allegations against Persico, revisiting his side's long-standing belief that the whole Colombo war was instigated by DeVecchio and Scarpa.

"We went through hell with the Snake article," he recalled. "But we were on point. It's a unique situation with the Persicos, goes way back to Scarpa. And you know, there's a lot of stuff and talking and bullshit, but the older you get, the more you can see the big picture, in the world and in life."

The uproar did little to change Little Vic's situation, and the Orenas continued to be opposed at every turn by authorities in their efforts to free their ailing patriarch.

Schoen, at an October 2021 hearing in Brooklyn federal court, described Little Vic as "a shell of a man." The one-time head of the Colombos was afflicted with Alzheimer's disease and convinced he was the warden of the facility where he was an inmate.

Court papers recounted the senior citizen firing his imaginary staff in "delusions accompanied with yelling, making demands and agitation."

Schoen, accompanied by Andrew Orena, echoed the assessment of the elderly inmate.

"Mr. Orena is completely unable to self-care," said the lawyer. "The delusions have been there for quite a while. Mr. Orena does not know who he is or where he is."

The convicted gangster contracted COVID-19 during the pandemic and later insisted that the whole crisis was conjured up by then-president Joe Biden. Orena was too weak to walk or even use the bathroom by himself, said Schoen. The lawyer then revisited the past and the decades-old Colombo war that landed Little Vic behind bars—again invoking DeVecchio's role in the violence.

"In the history of the FBI and the Justice Department, this misconduct in this case was unprecedented," he argued. "It's not as if we don't have a fully developed record of what happened there. The agent who testified as the expert witness in the Orena case was indicted for murder."

Assistant U.S. Attorney Devon Lash offered a different take on the conflict that pitted the Orenas against the Persicos, focusing on the carnage caused before the peace was established following multiple murders and mob arrests in arguing for his continued incarceration.

"He instigated a conflict that injured twenty-eight people and claimed [multiple] lives," she argued.

Federal judge Eric Komitee issued a ten-page ruling just two weeks later, reiterating Orena's medical issues: dementia, Alzheimer's, diabetes, glaucoma, hypertension, a pacemaker implanted in October 2009, and degenerative joint disease.

A list of the jailed Orena's daily medications was just as lengthy, with assorted pills to handle his growing health woes. A court filing noting that Little Vic's Alzheimer's treatment began in March 2018 was also noted.

"Due to his mental decline, Orena is said to receive 'a significant amount of redirection and reorientation,'" wrote Komitee.

"And his records from the past year reflect certain 'delusional episodes.'"

He then quoted from a federal court decision on a similar appeal from Vic's old mob associate John Gotti: "[A] defendant who meets all the criteria for compassionate consideration . . . is not thereby automatically entitled to sentence modification."

Gotti died June 10, 2002, inside the US Medical Center for Federal Prisoners in Springfield, Missouri. The flamboyant Dapper Don, age sixty-one, was 1,100 miles from his hometown, where he was returned for a last ride in a funeral cortege of nineteen cars carrying flowers and another twenty-two filled with mourners.

And Orena, like the high-profile and lethal Gotti, came with a lot of baggage from his time atop a New York crime family and his role in the deadly war, the judge wrote.

"A strain of cases has emerged in which the offender's criminal history is so long, and their victims so numerous, that even serious health conditions do no merit relief," continued Komitee. "This case falls squarely in that category."

While the judge left the door open for future appeals based on Orena's health woes, he slammed it shut for now.

"I am left with the inescapable conclusion that any sentence short of the life term imposed . . . would insufficiently reflect the seriousness of the offense conducted here and fail to provide just punishment," he declared.

Another bid for Orena's release in 2023 came with Schoen arguing that the prisoner merited a chance to die at home, an effort that again proved fruitless. A January 2024 court update noted that Orena was "admitted to a locked detention [four years earlier] due to his need for assistance in completing his activities of daily living, as well as because he was wandering. . . . He continues to need assistance with dressing himself."

The legal papers included a list of medical conditions that ran three pages long.

The Orena brothers never gave up hope, fighting the good fight for their father even as their one-time mob associates openly shared their memories of the old days for profit.

Mafia podcasts and videos became as common and constant as the sunrise, with an assortment of gangsters recounting their lives of crime for an audience still eager for the details of the mob's glory days and eventual demise. Combatant Larry Mazza wrote a book titled *The Life* and relocated to a comfortable new life as a personal trainer in Florida after nine years in a federal prison.

And there was the DeVecchio book. The long-retired federal agent remained adamant decades down the road that he did nothing wrong and had zero regrets.

"Not a one," he bluntly declared in a recent chat. "I loved every minute of it. I knew what I did, and what I didn't do. People can say what they want about me. At this stage in my life, I could care less. I'd do it all over again, probably the same way."

The Orena family, faced with the reality that their patriarch would likely die behind bars, refused to surrender as Little Vic's time behind bars stretched into a fourth decade, even as fellow combatants successfully argued for their own conditional releases.

War veteran Andrew Russo won his freedom in October 2021 after posting a $10 million bond in a case where he was accused in a Colombo family bid to seize control of a labor union. Defense attorneys argued that the eight-seven-year-old gangster no longer posed a threat to anyone because of his failing health, including a losing war with dementia. He died six months later while under house arrest. His attorney recounted how the cousin of Carmine Persico passed away surrounded by his loved ones.

Roughly one hundred mourners, including the gangster's granddaughter, filled Our Lady of Peace Church in Brooklyn for the send-off.

His colleague Anthony Russo, another Persico backer but no relation, applied for compassionate release and received a sentence reduction one year later, cutting his life term to thirty-five years. The Brooklyn federal court decision gave the septuagenarian hope for his freedom after serving another six years, in part for his role in the mob war murders of John Minerva and Michael Imbergamo.

The seventy-something Russo "has clearly demonstrated that he has achieved extraordinary rehabilitation," wrote federal judge Frederic Block in his decision after federal prosecutors argued against his release.

"The risk he poses [even at an advanced age] comes from the influence he has over others in the enterprise," said federal prosecutor Devon Lash in opposing the reduction.

Andrew Orena watched helplessly as his father's organized crime contemporaries walked free, resigned to the fact that Little Vic was destined to die behind bars.

"There's never going to be justice for my father," he said. "My father deserved a new trial. Everything that came out for my brothers with the Scarpa/DeVecchio stuff should have come out for my father, but it was suppressed."

The older Orena brothers would find their way back into mainstream life, their days in the mob a distant memory. Sixty-eight-year-old John, a retired father of two, still lives on Long Island. Sibling Vic Jr., sixty-seven, resettled in Sarasota, Florida, described by Andrew as in "good health, married with five children."

"It's a miracle that Johnny's home today and Vic's home with his family," said Andrew of his siblings. "Not only the possibility of getting killed in the war but the jail time. Everything that came out in that trial of my brothers should have come out for my father.

"I mean, there's never going to be justice for my father."

Andrew continues in his work as point man in the Orenas' losing battle, refusing to wave the white flag despite the repeated rebukes from prosecutors. Visiting the family patriarch became more difficult across the decades as Orena was moved to different prisons before landing in the Federal Medical Center in Devens, Massachusetts.

Despite all the years and the killings and betrayals, Andrew revealed, he reached out to the imprisoned Carmine Persico in a bid to mend the long-broken fences between the families turned frenemies about a decade before the boss's death.

"I wrote a nice letter to him," said Orena. "It was like an act of peace. It was when Allie Boy got convicted. I said, 'I really feel bad for Allie.' And I said, 'I never wanted to see the wrath and the path that happened to you and my dad.' And I said to him that I'm going to pray for him."

There was, he said, never any response from Junior.

Acknowledgments

Thanks to my wife Margie and our children Stacey, Megan, and Joe. A special shout-out to John and Andrew Orena for their time, help, and coffee while working on this book. Thanks to Frank Weimann and Gary Goldstein for their help and patience with this project. And thanks to all who made time to answer questions and provide some guidance on this book.